EDITED BY CHARLES EPTING

ORANGE COUNTY PIONEERS

ORAL HISTORIES FROM THE WORKS PROGRESS ADMINISTRATION

THE History PRESS

Published by The History Press
Charleston, SC 29403
www.historypress.net

First published 2014

Manufactured in the United States

ISBN 978.1.62619.758.9

Library of Congress Control Number: 2014952383

Notice: The information in this book is true and complete to the best of our knowledge. It is offered without guarantee on the part of the author or The History Press. The author and The History Press disclaim all liability in connection with the use of this book.

CONTENTS

INTRODUCTION

October 24, 1929, is a day that will always be remembered as "Black Thursday"—the day the stock market crashed and the county was plunged into a state of prolonged economic disaster. Although an apt politician, President Herbert Hoover (and his fellow Republican predecessors) were blamed by many for the situation. A few years later, Franklin Delano Roosevelt overwhelmingly won the 1932 presidential election on his promise of "a new deal for the American people."

It was these words—the "New Deal"—that came to embody the collective sum of President Roosevelt's relief programs during the Depression. Within his famed first one hundred days, Roosevelt established programs—such as the Civilian Conservation Corps (CCC) and the Federal Emergency Relief Administration (FERA)—that would go on to pave the way for the rest of his "Alphabet Soup Agencies."

It wouldn't be until April 8, 1935, that the New Deal's most well-known program was founded: the Works Progress Administration. Before the WPA was eventually dissolved in the middle of World War II (June 30, 1943), an estimated $13.4 billion was spent by the program across the nation. Employment figures are equally staggering; 8 million men and women were employed at various times during the program's eight-year history, with peak enrollment hitting 3.3 million at one time. There was hardly a city in the United States that was not affected by the WPA in some way.

The primary focus of the WPA was construction projects. The obvious goal of such projects was to provide unemployed breadwinners with steady jobs.

What the WPA also did with its improvement projects, however, was to provide civic infrastructure to parts of the nation that would not otherwise have been able to afford it. Works constructed included thousands of city halls, libraries, museums, bridges, sewers, irrigation channels and other such improvements.

There were also other facets of the WPA. Women, for example, were provided jobs sewing clothing, staffing nurseries and working in administrative offices. But more important to this work was Federal Project Number One, which was perhaps the most unique part of the WPA (and, consequently, is also one of the program's most enduring legacies).

Federal Project Number One was initially a collection of four programs that focused on providing out-of-work artists, writers, musicians and actors with employment. The fact that President Roosevelt and Harry Hopkins, the head of the WPA, included men and women in the arts in their relief program shows the immense amount of thought and planning behind the New Deal. As with construction projects, the benefits were twofold: men and women were employed by the programs, and small towns across the county benefitted from concerts, plays, murals, statues and books that would have never been created otherwise.

Few realize the sheer size of Los Angeles County when it was founded in 1850. At the time, California consisted of only twenty-seven counties (today there are fifty-eight). Parts or all of modern-day Orange, Kern, Riverside and San Bernardino Counties were originally part of Los Angeles County. *Author's collection.*

THE IDEA FOR THIS volume came while researching my recent book, *The New Deal in Orange County, California*. In tracking down all of the county's buildings from the New Deal, it was only a matter of time before I came across frequent references to the "Orange County Historical Research Project"—more formally known as WPA Project #3105.

Initially begun under the California State Emergency Relief Administration (SERA) in 1934, Project #3105 was a massive undertaking that sought to synthesize nearly everything that was known about Orange County's past at that time. About twenty-seven volumes were completed in total (the works are grouped differently in different repositories); topics include subjects as diverse as education, irrigation, government, religion, sports and architecture. Additionally, historical records—including the court case between Don Juan Forster and Pio Pico—were reproduced in their entirety. The Works Progress Administration completed the project between the years 1935 and 1937.

Over the years, the products of Project #3105 have been criticized by some as merely consisting of information copied from preexisting sources. While this is undeniably true to some extent, there is still a wealth of original information included in many of the volumes. Furthermore, in the time since Project #3105 was created, sources that were available to the WPA have been lost to history, increasing the value of the project.

My initial firsthand experience with Project #3105 came at the Orange County Archives in Santa Ana, where I found a photocopy of the volume

The current Santa Ana Public Library, dedicated in 1960, houses the Santa Ana History Room, which serves as a repository for the Work Progress Administration's Project #3105. Without its dedication to local history, this collection would not have been possible. *Courtesy the Santa Ana Public Library.*

titled *Adobes*. Although outdated, I recognized that the information contained in the book was invaluable. I spoke with historian Chris Jepsen, who works at the archives, about the project, and while he told me that they did not have a complete set of the volumes, the Santa Ana Public Library's History Room should have most (if not all) of the products of Project #3105.

Several library catalogue searches later, I found out that copies of some of the Project #3105 volumes were distributed across Southern California in addition to residing in the Santa Ana Library. University of California–Irvine, for example, has a complete set of copies, as well as the records of the

CALIFORNIA, THE MOTHER. ORANGE CO., THE CUB.

Orange County's separation from Los Angeles County in 1889 marked a dramatic decrease in the size of what was one of the state's original counties. After much debate, Santa Ana was chosen as the county seat due to both its size and location. Here, the new county is depicted as an affectionate cub of its mother, California. *Courtesy the Orange County Archives.*

archaeological work that the WPA undertook in Orange County. However, other than a complete index of the project compiled in the 1980s, both copies of the project and information about it are severely lacking.

At Jepsen's suggestion, I began visiting the Santa Ana Library History Room to read through the different volumes. While they all vary in length, each one contained information that made me look at the county in a new light. The one edition that stood out to me the most was called *Pioneer Tales*.

Pioneer Tales is a collection of interviews with Orange County's early settlers, many of whom moved to the county during the 1870s and 1880s. By the 1930s, these pioneers were elderly, but they still had no trouble recalling events that happened nearly half a century earlier. The mid-1930s were perhaps the last time in the county's history when so many pioneers were still alive and lucid about their experiences; the fact that the WPA was around to record their stories was a remarkable and serendipitous occurrence.

Between its pages were tales of bear hunts, bullfights, shootouts, lynchings and saloons. Initially, it was my intent to reproduce these stories to portray Orange County as a "Wild West" town, not that different than Dodge City or Tombstone. I began selecting excerpts that supported this view of Orange County. But I quickly learned in doing research on this book that what Project #3105 contained was much more important in portraying the early history of the county.

While many stories do indeed tell tales of daring adventures and dangerous outlaws, there are also a large number of anecdotes that recall what daily life was once like. To fully understand what Orange County was like during its pioneer days, the stories contained in *Pioneer Tales* must be taken in their entirety. While stories of hunting condors and lost pirate treasure are exciting, they are no more important that recollections of what early grocery stores were like, how the fledgling communities raised crops and livestock and how radically life changed when the railroads came in the 1870s.

The Federal Writers' Project (one of the Federal Project Number One programs) published hundreds of works across the United States during the New Deal. The most celebrated of these books were those of the American Guide Series, which included a guidebook for each of the forty-eight states at that time, as well as works for various territories, regions and cities. Within Southern California, books published included *San Diego: A California City*, *Los Angeles: A Guide to the City and Its Environs* and *Santa Barbara: A Guide to the Channel City and Its Environs*.

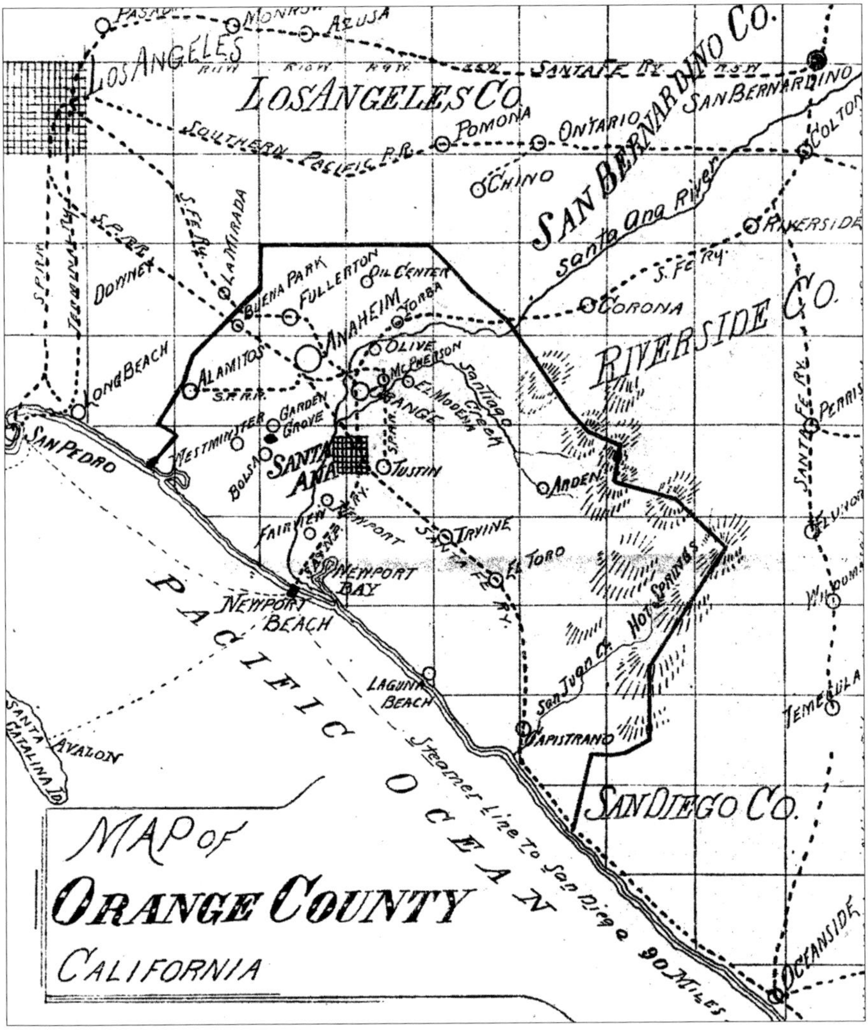

This early map of Orange County (circa 1900) shows many cities that are still prosperous today (for example, Anaheim, Santa Ana, Fullerton and Newport Beach). Other communities, such as Huntington Beach, have yet to be incorporated. The towns of Bolsa, McPherson, El Modena and El Toro have since been lost to history. *Courtesy the Orange County Archives.*

Orange County was never fortunate enough to receive a FWP book of its own, although the county is covered fairly extensively in the California statewide guide. However, there exists a book that serves as the inspiration and model for this work; in 1940, the Federal Writers' Project published a book titled *The Old West: Pioneer Tales of San Bernardino County*. Filled with whimsical illustrations and enthralling stories, the existence of an official

WPA book describing the pioneer tales of a neighboring county sets a precedent for this work.

This book reproduces many of the interviews from the WPA's Project #3105 volume *Pioneer Tales* as they originally were written. I have selected these specific passages because of their uniqueness, relevance and importance; however, there was far too much contained in the original volume for every passage to be reproduced herein. Therefore, this book should not be considered a republishing of the WPA's work but rather a curated collection of stories rearranged and edited to form a cohesive narrative.

I have attempted to reproduce the text as exactly as possible. In some cases, however, I have changed spelling and grammar for the sake of consistency and modernity (for example, "tonight" instead of "to-night" and "Indian" instead of "indian"). In doing this, I have retained the original intention and meaning of the text as nearly as possible. I have also removed certain irrelevant segments of text from some of the interviews in order to make the stories more concise. It must be remembered that these writings are nearly eighty years old at the time of this publication. Writing conventions have changed in that time, so a certain amount of editorial oversight was necessary to modernize the work.

I have also made editorial decisions to exclude certain passages due to their offensive subject matter. Social norms have changed greatly since the nineteenth century, and for this reason, stories that are excessively racist, sexist or violent have been omitted.

It is my hope that someday the entirety of Project #3105 will be republished; however, given the extensive nature of the project (I cannot even hazard a guess as to the word count for all of the volumes combined), this is an ambitious goal at best. By reprinting these stories from *Pioneer Tales*, perhaps some interest in the project will be rekindled, and more attention will be paid to the works of the WPA.

I would like to close by saying that I like to think of this book as a continuation of President Franklin Roosevelt's New Deal philosophy. Roosevelt's programs were extremely controversial in their day and remain so today. The WPA had supporters and naysayers from both sides of the aisle. But while the New Deal as a whole remains a contentious historical issue, what cannot be denied are the extensive contributions that the art programs of Federal Project Number One left behind. Federal Art Project murals still adorn many civic buildings, and the American Guide Series is still considered a masterpiece by book collectors.

INTRODUCTION

It is my goal that this book follows in the footsteps of the guidebooks compiled by the Federal Writers' Project under President Roosevelt's Works Progress Administration.

ORIGINAL PREFACE

Honor is due the names of those courageous men and women who dared the hazards of the overland trail or the perilous sea voyage to blaze a path and establish a civilization for future generations.

It seems eminently fitting that the names and experiences of Orange County's Pioneers should be perpetuated in such a manner that their labor in the days of trial and hardship may remain an inspiration to the people of today.

To come into contact with a man or woman who has left the impress of his intellect, personality and perseverance upon his locality, or to peruse an account of his useful life is to be helped in a practical and impressive manner.

It is therefore the object of these compilations to present a true picture of pioneer days by preserving the narratives so graciously and willingly given us by the participants themselves or their immediate descendants.

Some excerpts from old books and histories have been added occasionally to facilitate continuity.

Mrs. G.E. Ashby, Project Supervisor
U.S. Works Progress Administration Project #3105

Chapter 1

SANTA ANA

Santa Ana was founded in 1869, when Mr. William H. Spurgeon purchased seventy-six acres of land that was nothing more than a sycamore grove. As soon as he arrived at his land, Mr. Spurgeon climbed to the top of one of the numerous sycamore trees in order to survey his property; little did he know that the town he was about to lay out would become one of Southern California's largest cities. Although the tree Spurgeon climbed was chopped down many years ago, a plaque stands at Fifth Street and the aptly named Sycamore Street to commemorate the city's somewhat mythological founding.

In the WPA's *Pioneer Tales* volume, there exists a great wealth of information about Santa Ana in the decades after Spurgeon first climbed that tree. During the mid-1930s, many men and women who moved to the area in the 1870s and 1880s were still alive to recall the city's first school, telegraph and library. A large number of anecdotes also revolve around the region's rich agricultural history.

The following passages were selected in an attempt to give a comprehensive overview of Santa Ana's earliest days. Let the words of these pioneers take you on a journey through Santa Ana at a time when horses still roamed wild and there was only a one-room schoolhouse for all of the city's children.

Reminisces of Early Santa Ana

Perhaps the most important account of life in early Santa Ana contained in the WPA volumes was given by E.P. Stafford, who came to the city as a young child and would go on to be a banker. Stafford's father was one of the city's first prominent residents and was integral in implementing much of Santa Ana's infrastructure. Here, in abbreviated form, is Stafford's recollection of what the town was once like.

I have been asked to give a little history on the early City as I remember it.

In the summer of 1868 father took a vacation and came south to Los Angeles County. The Rancho Santiago de Santa Ana was just being subdivided at the time, and he made an offer to buy the interest of one of the heirs, and his offer was accepted. He returned to Petaluma and was telling his friend, a man by the name of Columbus Tustin of his purchase. Mr. Tustin asked father if he might not take a half interest, which was agreed to.

In the summer of 1873, father loaded a large lumber wagon (known in those days as a California lumber wagon, with a high seat mounted on springs fully six feet or more above the ground) with much of his household goods. Behind this he attached a spring wagon, commonly used in those days, with more furniture, on top of which he arranged a bed. To these wagons he hitched four horses, and he, together with two of my bothers, one older and one younger than myself, and I climbed aboard and started a long, perilous journey, consuming twenty-one days' time, over rough, dusty roads, very mountainous in many places; often for several days drinking alkali or sulphur water, depending on finding feed by the wayside for our team, cooking our meals over a campfire

William H. Spurgeon (1829–1915), the founder of Santa Ana, is still memorialized with the name of a street in that city. After purchasing the land, Spurgeon climbed a tree to survey the surrounding lots; the city he envisioned would go on to become the county seat. Few men, if any, were as influential in the early development of the region. *Courtesy Santa Ana Public Library.*

mornings and evenings, eating a cold lunch on the wagon at noon. Some days we would not make more than fifteen or twenty miles. Other days, where the traveling was good, we would cover thirty miles or more, and after traveling between 500 and 600 miles we arrived safely in Santa Ana.

While I was only a lad of eleven years, many of the happenings en route stand out as clear in my memory as though it was but yesterday. We followed the road used by the stage. (The railroad was just being built from San Francisco to Los Angels at that time. The construction crew were working in the Salinas Valley, and I remember well watching the engine moving the rails and ties on the flat cars ahead of the locomotive, the men placing the ties and nailing the rails in place and then pushing the cars forward with very little loss of time. The roadbed had been constructed for many miles in advance.)

The stage made daily trips before the railroad was constructed between San Francisco and Los Angeles. Father usually wrote a letter to mother each evening and would hand it to the stage driver as they would pass, thus keeping mother in touch as to where we were. There were relay stations about twenty or twenty-five miles apart along the route where the stage horses were exchanged for fresh horses, and usually we would try to stop over night at one of these places as food for ourselves and our team could be purchased. If we could not get to a relay station, we would try to find a farmhouse at which to camp. Very often we would be compelled to strike camp at 2 or 3 o'clock in the afternoon as it would be many miles to the next water.

After leaving the Salinas Valley we traveled through a mountainous pass and camped at a relay station called Ballard. There was a toll road at this place over the mountain to Santa Barbara. We were told that this road was very steep in places so we continued down through Gaviota Pass to the ocean. I remember this pass most distinctly because I was so badly scared when passing through the narrows where the rocks seemed to come almost together overhead and I was afraid they would break loose and fall on us.

It was certainly a beautiful sight on passing through to come in sight of the ocean.

That night we stopped at a Spanish house located in a deep arroyo coming down from the mountain in which flooded a nice stream of good water.

The man of the house was away and the lady could not speak English but father could speak their language very fluently. She let us have hay, milk, and some eggs. We cross the stream and drew the wagon to the side of the road and prepared our beds for the night. My older brother and I always slept on the ground and father and my younger brother occupied the bed on the trail wagon.

I remember this camp so well because we were just clearing up after our evening meal when we noticed a number of horsemen coming down the road we just traveled. They drew rein at the farm house and all went in. They remained possibly half an hour or more and then came out, mounted their horses and came on past where we were. I was sitting on the tongue of the wagon and they passed within six feet of where I sat. The leader was riding a beautiful grey horse, and said his name was Vasquez. Father said he saw him at a trial in San Rafael, Marin County, where he had been convicted for horse stealing. Several days later, when we arrived at Santa Barbara, we learned it was a band of desperados headed by Vasquez, and that they had committed murder and robbed a store at Tres Pinas three days previous to our seeing them.

Another thing that stands out so clearly in my memory is our arrival at Los Angeles, then a city of only a few thousand, possibly five or six thousand inhabitants. We camped in Cahuenga Pass Saturday night, left early Sunday morning, passed through what is now Hollywood, at that time a pasture covered with herds of wild cattle. Our route led down Temple Street until we got almost to the city and over to Sunset Boulevard down past the old Mission at the Plaza, and we drew our team up at a watering trough at the old Pico House located on the gore lot at the intersection of Main and Los Angeles Streets, just opposite the Mission. I was particularly impressed at seeing all the Mexican people lift their hats and bare their heads while passing the Church.

We camped Sunday night at the Seventeen Mile house, another relay station between Los Angeles and San Diego. The next day, Monday, we arrived in Santa Ana, drawing up at Spurgeon Brothers' store located at that time west of Broadway, then West Street at the intersection of Fourth Street. This was the end of Fourth Street at that time, everything west of Broadway being acreage. It was about three o'clock in the afternoon when we arrived. The Post Office was located in the store, Mr. W.H. Spurgeon being postmaster. Father got what little mail there was for us and then we continued on to Mr. Tustin's home for the night.

We crossed the Santa Ana River and what was known as the Bates Crossing, so named because Mr. Bates lived on the river at this point. This crossing was located about a mile or less below the present Santa Ana Boulevard Crossing. The main crossing of the river was at the Roderiquez Crossing, often spoken of as the Lockhart Crossing, so named because of

Fourth Street, one of Santa Ana's main thoroughfares, in 1891. *Courtesy the Orange County Archives.*

the old adobe of Roderiquez afterwards purchased from Mr. Lockhart. This crossing was located less than a mile above the Santa Ana Boulevard.

On our arrival in Santa Ana, father sent for mother, who followed by steamer, which anchored at sea off San Pedro. Passengers and their luggage were taken ashore in a small tug boat. We at once began construction of a home. Our house was built on what is now Walnut Street, just east of Orange Avenue and our barn was built in the middle of what is now Orange Avenue at a point about 150 feet south of Walnut Street. The old home was moved a number of times after father's death to make room for subdivision of this section, and is now located on the west side of Artesia Street at West Eighth Street, and is being used by the colored people as the Second Baptist Church.

It was in this home that the first telegraph office was located from May, 1875 until June, 1877. The instruments were in our dining room and were in the charge of mother. She knew but little about telegraphy and was a little reluctant about accepting the responsibility of taking charge, but the company's superintendent at Los Angeles persuaded her that she would have very little trouble. Her first instrument had a tape on which the dots and dashes registered and it was possible for any one acquainted with the code to read the messages as they were recorded.

It was only a short time, however, until mother was taking everything by sound. Many of the messages were for the San Joaquin Rancho or the McFadden brothers, and I was privileged to pick up many quarters for delivering same. The telegraph line running between Los Angeles and San Diego followed the old stage road. This road passed through Anaheim, coming in on what is now Center Street to Los Angeles Street and continuing south for possibly two miles and then taking a southeasterly direction crossing the river at the Roderiguez's adobe home, from thence across the Santiago Creek at a point about where the Santa Fe Railway crosses, on to the San Joaquin Rancho just east of Tustin, at which place there was an old adobe used as a relay station, where the stage horses were exchanged for fresh ones. This road was about a mile and a half northeast of Santa Ana, and it was to this point that the telegraph company built a loop to tap the old wires.

There were many old adobes in what is now Orange County, at that time a part of Los Angeles County. These adobes were in a good state of preservation and were occupied by many of the old Spanish families.

The Sepulveda family lived in one of these houses located about a quarter of a mile west of Bristol Street and about the same distance south of First Street. The main living room was on the north, and then there was an annex extending to the south which was used first for help and then as a storeroom and a harness and saddle room, and last a room for horses.

There was a trail leading from the Gabe Allen adobe located about five miles to the southwest near Fairview. This trail continued in a northeasterly direction to the Bates home, another adobe located at the Bates Crossing on the Santa Ana River, from this point to the Roderiguez home, continuing on to the Tom Mott home, later known as the Fletcher adobe; from there up the Santa Ana Canyon to Peralta and Yorba Peralta was called in those days, "Upper Santa Ana." This trail was very pronounced, having been traveled for many years, and as time went on the winds in the rain would carry the dust out until in many places it was three or four feet deep.

After father had established a home, he cleaned the mustard that grew ten feet high or higher over our entire ranch, and begin raising grain, such as barley, rye, corn and alfalfa. It was uphill business as the Mexicans would herd their cattle over the fields at night and destroy the crops. However, in 1874, Noah Palmer and a company of friends came to Santa Ana from Santa Clara County and purchased the Sepulveda grant which lay just across Main Street from our home. After Mr. Palmer came, the Spaniards moved away, so we had no further trouble. I wish to say in passing that I attended a gathering at which a picture of the Roderiguez adobe was thrown on the screen, all dotted up with green trees in a very beautiful setting. For fear one would get a wrong idea, I can remember this building very well, and in the early days, it, like most of them, had very little growth around. Many of them had been whitewashed, but, in most cases the whitewash had scaled badly, while others lacked any dressing whatsoever. Usually they stood out in the open with the hot sun beating down, and if there were trees nearby, they were generally olive trees. Some had tile roofs, but most of them were thatched. The floors were mostly earth, but always swept very clean. Many had covered porches on which the people would gather.

The people were very hospitable, and one was never turned away hungry or without shelter at night. They gave very little trouble other than pasturing their stock on your grain fields. They occasionally fought with knives among themselves, but seldom attack the whites unless they were drunk. They traveled mostly on horseback in companies of a dozen or more and the horses moved in a little dog trot. Often the old women would be conveyed from place to place in homemade two-wheel carts drawn by oxen. I have seen many of these old cards, some with canopies covered with burlap; the wheels were of solid wood. They were always kind to the old. The young men were very expert with the reata, which they made from rawhide of their own tanning. They also made hair ropes from the mane and tail of the

The caption of this photograph simply identifies the men as "vaqueros" in Santa Ana, circa 1880. The image is a reminder of Orange County's truly "Wild West" history, complete with bandits, gunfights and saloons. *Courtesy the Santa Ana Public Library.*

mustang horses which grazed on the prairies in great numbers. The natives would spend their last cent for silver trimmings for their saddles and bridles, many of which were worth over a hundred dollars. The better class of Spaniards drove very fine teams. They used the spring wagons so common in the early days.

Artesian wells, such as the one seen here, were invaluable to Orange County's pioneers, in many cases providing them with their sole sources of water. Philanthropic members of the community would often make their water available to neighbors. *Courtesy the Anaheim Public Library.*

When the white settlers moved in, they raised much barley, corn, and other grain, most of which was marketed in San Francisco, being shipped by boat via Anaheim Landing. The larger vessels would anchor at sea, when weather permitted, and the grain would be lightered out in flat bottom boats.

Later the McFadden brothers (James and Robert) had a small steamer built which they named "The Newport" and much of the produce was shipped from Newport Harbor. The steamer "Newport" plied between that port and San Francisco, carrying merchandise south and grain north. The McFaddens also shipped most of our lumber in after building their boat. Their yard was located on the high ground immediately back of the Baptist Church on Main Street. Prior to this, much of her lumber came via Anaheim Landing or was milled in the San Bernardino mountains.

As I mentioned before, the Spurgeon brothers ran the only store. They also drilled an artesian well on the lot now occupied by the Spurgeon Building. This was a flowing well and was the nucleus of the first water system of Santa Ana constructed by the Spurgeons; and when the City installed our present system the Spurgeon plant was purchased.

Due to Southern California's naturally dry climate, steady access to water was always a primary concern. It wouldn't be until the Los Angeles Aqueduct was completed in 1913 that many of the Southland's residents no longer had to worry about securing their own water from wells or rivers.

Santa Ana was quite a place for buggy riding and had many livery stables. The first to be erected was built by Jim Hickey on the northwest corner of Fourth and Sycamore Streets, the present site of the Rossmore Hotel [no longer standing]. In order to secure a conveyance of any kind, one would have to engage his team many days in advance, often as much as two weeks. It was in front of this stable I saw Mr. Titchenal, then town constable, shot. John Nemo had a saloon on the northeast corner of Fourth and Sycamore Streets on the lot now occupied by the Rankin Drygoods Company, noted for being quite a gambling den and in which many fights occurred. It was in the middle 70's or possibly 76 or 77 that one Ike McManus got into a quarrel and Mr. Titchenal was called. McManus was informed, and he ran to the Hickey barn for his saddle horse. Titchenal arrived on the scene just as McManus was coming out and he, Titchenal, grabbed the horse's bridal and raised his cane which he always carried, when Mc pulled his gun and shot, the bullet striking just below the stomach, passing through the upper leg. Mr. Birch, one of the early settlers and for whom Birch Park was named, ran to the rescue and caught Titchenal as he was falling. A number of men assisted and carried the wounded man to the Cummings Drug Store located on the north side

Fourth Street in Santa Ana, 1889. Streetcar tracks run down the middle of the dirt street, while numerous horse-drawn carriages are parked on either side of the road. *Courtesy the Orange County Archives.*

of Forth about where Vic Walker's Sporting store is now located. A little later they carried into his home on the lot now occupied by the First National Bank.

The *Los Angeles Herald* reported on June 22, 1876, that "Constable Titchenal, of Santa Ana, was shot in the leg Tuesday [June 20] while attempting to arrest a man for disturbing the peace." The injury reportedly crippled William Titchenal for life.

The first church building erected was built on the present site of the Baptist Church by that denomination in 1876. It was a frame structure and when first used was unfinished inside, not being plastered, but all the studdings and rafters were bare. The seats were 2x12 plank planes without backs, except two or three rows in front which had 6 inch boards nailed on strips attached to the planks. These planks were set on nail kegs. My father died in June, 1878, and the services were conducted in this church by Rev. Parker, one of the early pastors. Prior to this time church services were held in the first schoolhouse built in Santa Ana.

The first public school was opened in 1870 and was held in a small room in a house located on the northwest corner of Fifth and Main Streets. One of the first and probably the first teacher was Miss Anna Cozad. Her parents lived on the southeast corner of Main and McFadden Streets, afterwards the home of James McFadden.

> *Mr. W.W. Johnson, son of Squire Johnson, attended school in this building. However, he and Mrs. W.H. Spurgeon both told me that they were of the opinion that this was a private school; but be that as it may, I am thoroughly convinced that the first building erected, specifically for school purposes, was built in 1870 and was located on the northeast corner of Church and Broadway on the lot now occupied by the Spurgeon Memorial M.E. Church, South.*

The site of the first schoolhouse is now immediately west of the old YMCA building; because the roads have been rerouted, the school would have stood in the middle of Civic Center Drive.

> *This was a one-room structure, possibly 35 or 40 feet long by 20 feet wide. It was in this building I first attended school in 1873. The first teacher I can remember was Prof. Brown, followed by Prof. Hewitt, who was the son-in-law of Noah Palmer, and he was followed by Prof. Cyrus Andrews. Mr. Andrews did not teach in the first school building but came shortly after the second building was erected. The first school was provided with seats and desks made to accommodate two pupils. There were three rows*

One of Santa Ana's first public schools, photographed in the early 1890s. During the city's early history, classes were often conducted in local homes when more formal facilities were not available. *Courtesy California State University, Fullerton.*

of the seats, possibly twelve in each row, and would accommodate about 70 students.

When I first attended the school the room was not more than half full, and the children in some cases came from long distances, some from Delhi, others from two or more miles. I can call to mind Loftus Russell, who lived two or more miles to the northeast, Martha Robinson, now Mrs. M.E. Ritchey, living at least two miles to the southeast, and by the way, Mrs. Ritchey is living in the same vicinity now that she lived sixty-five years ago. Will and Jesse Vance and Ralph Gage came more than a mile and a half. We had no automobiles in those days but most of us walked. One or two had saddle horses; I think Mrs. Ritchey rode.

In those days Santa Ana had a good healthy growth, and by 1875 the room was filled to capacity. It became apparent that one teacher could not handle all the pupils, so the school, trustees, one of whom was Dr. Greenleaf, father of Walter and Bob Greenleaf who are still living in the city, looked for accommodations for the younger children. There was a vacant building on the northeast corner of Fifth and Main Streets, erected for a blacksmith shop, with rooms overhead and a stairway leading up on the outside of the building. These rooms were rented and a teacher was provided for the little fellows. In 1876, it was decided to build more commodious quarters. This promulgated quite an argument as some of the citizens thought it best to construct a four-room structure while others argued that it was a waste of money, as they said Santa Ana would never require a four-room building. I remember my father suggested they build a four-room school with two rooms on the ground and two rooms above and that they furnish the two lower rooms only. This seemed to meet with the approval of most people and the district proceeded to erect a building on Church Street at the head of Sycamore Street. This was in the year 1876. Church Street at that time was the northern boundary of Santa Ana. As you stood on the steps of this school you faced down the center of Sycamore Street. This building has been moved two or three times and is now located immediately north of the YMCA tennis court on the west side of Sycamore Street.

On the completion of the second school building, the old schoolhouse, located on the lot now occupied by the M.E. Church, South, was sawed in two, one half being moved to Delhi, the other half was moved to the Diamond district west of Bristol Street on the north side of Edinger Street, and they were both fitted up for school rooms, thereby reducing the territory for Santa Ana to draw from.

Delhi was a community centered near Warner Avenue (formerly called Delhi Road) and Main Street, south of downtown Santa Ana. The Delhi School District operated from 1879 to 1924. Located slightly to the northwest of Delhi was Diamond, a school district founded in 1877. There is still a Diamond Elementary School located at Edinger Avenue and Greenville Street.

> *Before leaving the school, I would like to relate one or two of the amusing incidents that occurred in this room. It was while Prof. Brown was schoolmaster. Many of the older boys were larger than the teacher, and in some cases were unruly, but Brown was equal to the occasion. I remember one fellow, Jack Faulkner by name, gave the teacher some trouble and Brown took him to account for some mischief he had committed. Faulkner tried to put Brown out of the house. Being a big, strong boy, he was a little too much for Brown and he pushed him down one aisle of the room to the entrance which was in the rear of the building; but by this time he reached the door, Faulkner was well winded, but Brown, being more mature, was just getting into action, and instead of passing out the door, he slowed Faulkner, passed and marched him up the other aisle to the rostrum where he sat down and proceeded to punish him. Well they got along very nicely after that.*
>
> *On another occasion, as school was closing for the day, Dave Titchenal, who is quite a hand to pick on the smaller fellow, took it into his head to abuse a fellow by the name of Ralph Gage. Gage was a big, powerful fellow, strong as an ox, but backward, timid, and very bashful. Ralph was carrying a slate, one of the kind we used in those days made of stone and with a wooden frame. Dave said, "Hold up your slate, Ralph," and Ralph, not suspecting anything, obeyed. Well, Dave drove his fist through the slate and smashed into thousand pieces. Well, did he stir up a hornets nest? I say he did. Ralph grabbed him by the back of the neck and the seat of his trousers and marched him over to an irrigation ditch that ran along the school lot and threw him in, shoved his head under the water, and would probably have drowned him if about four or five of the other boys had not rescued him. Needless to say, Ralph was never bothered in the future.*
>
> *Prof. Andrews assumed charge of the school shortly after moving and was well liked by all. He had a very unfortunate experience in Santa Ana. He purchased a ranch in the Delhi district, drilled a well for artesian water and got more than he bargained for. Many of the old timers will remember this well. It could not be controlled. When it was capped it broke outside of the pipe and flooded everybody near. Ranch owners in the neighborhood threatened to sue Andrews and the*

poor fellow was doing all he could to control the water. I believe he finally gave his ranch away to get rid of the water.

Getting back to the school, the attendance grew so rapidly it was but a short time until it became necessary to furnish the two upper rooms and employ four teachers.

My father died in 1878, and this ended my school activities. I never got past the eighth grade.

There seems to be some diversity of opinion as to when the first high school class graduated. Through the assistance of my mother, Mrs. R.J. Blee, I am able to furnish some facts. In 1891 there was a class of three boys, Harry Hunt, Lee McDill and my brother, Walter Stafford, graduated under Prof. J.N. Keram, as principal. These boys had taken the regular course of studies taught in the high schools throughout the State. All passed with good credits and were admitted to the Leland Stanford University at Palo Alto on the certificates issued by the Santa Ana school at the time. (This was the year Stanford was opened.) My brother finished his work in that University and received his diploma with the first full time class graduating from that institution, so naturally we old timers forgot the class of '91 is the first high school class of Santa Ana. However, the Santa Ana High School was not accredited by the state universities until two years later, so, properly speaking, I suppose the class of '93 can claim the distinction of being the first high school class. The class of '91 probably would not have been able to enter Berkeley, but Stanford was just opening and was not under the supervision of the State.

Founded in 1889, Santa Ana High School was the first high school to be established in Orange County (coincidentally, this was the same year that Orange County achieved independence from Los Angeles).

I attended the graduating exercises of the class of '91 in the Spurgeon Hall, located on the second floor of the brick building that was torn down to make room for the present Spurgeon Building on the southwest corner of Fourth and Sycamore Streets.

A number of years later, the first high school was built on the east side of Main Street, between Ninth and Tenth Streets. This structure was but recently torn down. Where the present Polytechnic High School now stands was an open field as late as 1906, and it was on this field that Glenn Martin tried his first airplane. I, with my family and many others, went down to see him test his first plane. He ran around the ground a number of

This 1904 image shows one of Santa Ana High School's early graduating classes. The first high school in the county, its establishment gave the city of Santa Ana legitimacy in the eyes of Los Angeles and helped propel the area into a more modern way of life. *Courtesy the Santa Ana Public Library.*

times but she just would not fly. However, later I had the pleasure of seeing him take off from the same field with his mother and father as passengers.

One of America's aviation pioneers, Glenn Martin's surname is forever immortalized by the Lockheed Martin company. Martin, a kite enthusiast from the Midwest, was inspired by the Wright brothers to experiment with aviation. In 1909, he constructed his first plane—the one that Mr. Stafford went to see—which was destroyed before leaving the ground. In 1912, Martin made the first water-to-water flight, from Balboa to Catalina Island and back, and several years later, he founded one of the most successful aviation companies in the nation.

There were many very beautiful sycamore trees that were so plentiful in the early days of Santa Ana. Many of these grand old trees were several hundred years old and measured four and five feet in diameter. Often these trees grew in groups of a dozen or more, and it was the exception, rather

Glenn Martin, one of aviation's true pioneers, developed his first airplane while living in Santa Ana. He would achieve fame with the first water-to-water flight in history, from Balboa to Catalina Island, in 1912. *Courtesy the Orange County Archives.*

than the rule, to see one standing alone. I don't know of any of the old trees being left in Santa Ana. Sycamore Street derived its name from grand old sycamores along its path. Mr. and Mrs. English, parents of the late Mrs. Spurgeon, built their home under the broad branches of a number of these trees on the east side of Sycamore Street between Second and Third Streets. Mr. Titchenal, one of the early peace officers of Santa Ana, had his home on the present site of the First National Bank, located on the southwest corner of Main and Fourth Streets, under four or more very fine sycamores.

Each of these trees had a spread of a hundred feet or more and would measure five feet in diameter at the truck. There were twenty or more very large trees around the home of Mr. John Bush, located about where Church Street would intersect French if Church were extended eastward to that point.

I have often thought what a wonderful park this grove would have made for Santa Ana, and twenty acres could have been purchased for a very nominal figure before this section was subdivided into town lots. Speaking of a park, I wonder how many people of Santa Ana know that the public minded ladies of Santa Ana secured an option of the two blocks located between Main Street on the east, and Broadway on the west, running from Sixth Street to Church Street. These ladies gave a number of entertainments

Landmarks in this circa 1876 bird's-eye view of Santa Ana include two churches, the Odd Fellows' Hall, the Santa Ana Hotel and Sycamore Hall. In the distance, the Santa Ana and San Bernardino Mountains tower over the landscape. Today, the vast fields that can be seen in the lithograph have been completely destroyed. *Courtesy the University of California.*

and secured enough money to make a down payment, but were unable to raise sufficient funds to consummate the deal. To verify this statement I refer you to "A Bird's-eye View of Santa Ana" published in the late 70's which shows these two blocks all landscaped for a park.

The first railroad built by the Southern Pacific Company arrived in Los Angeles in 1875 and was extended to Anaheim, which was the terminus until March, 1878, at which time it was built into Santa Ana. They had quite extensive stockyards at the station which stood on Fruit Street and I have stood in the door of our home on Orange and Walnut Avenues and watch them load cattle trains. There were many, many trains sent out of Santa Ana.

As I have said, we were engaged in raising grain principally. I spoke of the Spaniards herding their stock on our grain fields. Another thing we had to contend with were the wild geese and ducks which came in by the thousands. I am a little reluctant about saying how many, but I can only say, we measured them by acres and not by numbers, and this is not a fish story. The ground would be white with the wild geese in the fall of the year. It was no trouble to get a good fat goose for dinner any time. Other game was plentiful also, such as quail and cotton-tail rabbits. There were also many deer in the nearby hills. The late Parker brothers, Ed and Clarence, hunted for the market and shipped much game to Los Angeles.

Mule teams such as this one were instrumental in transporting crops and other goods throughout the county. The coming of the railroad in the 1870s rendered many of them obsolete, although they continued to serve the county's more rural parts. *Courtesy the Santa Ana Public Library.*

The coyotes and badgers were also very plentiful. We raised some chickens and turkeys for our own use and the badgers would burrow into the yards and steal our chickens. The coyotes would keep up a continuous yelping most of the night, but one would become used to it and sleep as soundly as though it were quiet.

The people had but little money but needed less. We wore plain clothing such, as a pair of overalls and a work shirt for the men, and homemade clothing for the ladies. In fact, my mother made most of the clothing for us boys and as we went barefoot we did not buy shoes. I have seen many of the older men without shoes, but we were most contented. Everybody knew each other for miles around and we had many pleasant times together. Someone would make it known that they wished to entertain. The word would go out and everybody would come, no invitations necessary. Usually food was served, followed by music and singing. The most outstanding entertainers were Mr. and Mrs. James Rice. She was a great singer and one of the favorite songs was "The Mocking Bird." Mrs. Rice would sing to her own accompaniment and he would whistle just like the mocking bird. Never a Fourth of July or a May Day passed without a picnic or a barbecue. Some of the favorite places of gatherings was the present Irvine

Park, not named, however, at that time, or large sycamore grove in the eastern limits of Tustin when the McFadden pasture at the foot of Bristol Street.

It just seems to me the most hospitable people on earth were the old frontier families. Never did they turn a fellow away hungry and yet it seems that no one was ever imposed on.

I am inclined to think I could go on indefinitely writing of the early history of our community. There was such a lack of malice or hatred among each other.

I have left unsaid many of my pleasant remembrances.

Santa Ana's First Telegraph

Mrs. R.J. Blee, mother of E.P. Stafford and one of the most prominent women in early Santa Ana, also had something to say about her time as Santa Ana's first telegraphist.

> *In 1874 my brother, Henry, who is a court reporter in Los Angeles, brought down a telegraph instrument as a Christmas present to the boys with the idea that they might possibly fit themselves to become telegraphers. I became more interested than the boys and practiced the Morse code at every opportunity until I had really learned it. As Santa Ana had no telegraph office then, it was suggested that I were to take over the responsibility of becoming the operator. At first I hesitated because I had so many other duties. When the company agreed to put in a register to record the messages while I was away from the instrument, I decided to take over the work. I received half of the receipt of the officers compensation and held the position for two years and one month.*
>
> *At the start there was no money in it, of course, but when the local merchants came to use the telegraph more and more to place their orders business increased until I made quite a sum for my work.*
>
> *I remember that I just started my work as telegrapher when the Hayes-Tilden presidential election* [of 1876] *took place and I was rather proud of myself when I managed to do all of the telegraph work connected with the election returns.*

Communication in Orange County would become much easier a few years later, when the Southern Pacific Railroad connected Santa Ana to the rest of Southern California.

Peanut and Chili Growing

Mr. Michael Witt immigrated to Wisconsin from Germany in 1869; thirteen years later, Witt, his wife and their children decided to try their hand at farming in Orange County. A prominent member of the German Evangelical Church in Santa Ana, Witt quickly acquired land throughout the county and became one of the county's most notable farmers. In 1936, he reflected on some of the early crops that he grew after first moving to California—the first of which is not typically associated with Orange County.

> *When the Santiago Creek overflowed a sediment deposit was left which was fine for peanut growing, much in the way that the James River fertilizes the soil of Virginia. This land being seated for the ground peanuts, I started a peanut farm.*
>
> *Some years I harvested two thousand sacks. These were at first sent to San Francisco from Newport. Some years were bad years, and in one such year I shipped five hundred pounds by car to San Francisco, receiving only two and one half cents per pound. As this did not pay the expense of raising the product, I stored the remainder in my barn, and received five cents a pound from peanut vendors in Los Angeles, who bought fifty sacks each month. These vendors had small stores along the streets and roasted peanuts, like chestnuts are roasted in San Francisco over charcoal fires.*
>
> *After the ground had been cultivated, the peanuts were sown in April and we never irrigated. They were the large Santa Ana humpback variety. When the peanuts were mature, the vines were cut with a large knife which was three feet long with fingers riveted into it. This knife raised the vines up. They were left on the ground for three or four days to dry so that the dirt would not cake to the nuts. Then they were stacked in a pile and picked by hand.*
>
> *Mr. Ed Utt improved on this method of harvesting. He had a gasoline engine, which was rigged to an elevator twelve feet long. In the belt of the contraption there were inch square holes through which the peanuts fell into a container while the fingers of the knife pulled off the vines which clung to the nuts. This method could handle large quantities of nuts, and Mr. Utt had sixteen thousand sacks of peanuts at one time.*
>
> *I also raised peanuts on rented land between Tustin and Santa Ana, and was known as "the Peanut King."*

For decades afterward, many old-timers fondly remembered Mr. Utt's extensive peanut fields in Tustin, which Witt claimed were a direct result of

Mr. C.E. Utt of Tustin was one of the most notable peanut growers in early Orange County. Here, his shop is seen, with one of the area's early streetcars running in front. Peanuts no longer serve as a viable cash crop in the region. *Courtesy the Los Angeles Public Library.*

his own success with the crop. In those days, Utt's products were advertised as "double-jointed goober peas." Although peanuts are no longer grown commercially in the county, they represented a very important cash crop up until the 1930s.

Michael Witt also recalled another of his horticultural endeavors: chilies.

> *On the land at Katella, I raised chilies. These were sown in warm beds in late February or March. They were gathered dream in October, and put into a house with a furnace and dried. Each chili was suspended by a string sewed through the green end. I dried ten tons of peppers at one time. Ten tons of green peppers made five tons of dried ones. Most of my chili crop was sent to Los Angeles, and from there they were sent especially to Texas and New Mexico and Arizona.*

The peppers that Witt grew were Anaheim chilies, so named because a man named Emilio Ortega introduced the variety to Anaheim from New Mexico in 1894. Today, the Ortega Mexican food company still uses green Anaheim chilies in its line of salsas.

The First American Child Born in Santa Ana

A letter from Mrs. Walter Everts in 1934 described a debate in the community regarding the identity of the first American child to be born in Santa Ana. In it, she identifies two primary candidates for the title.

> *There is a great difference of opinion among the early residents of Santa Ana as to who was the first American child born here.*
>
> *Tom Harlin, son of Thomas Jefferson (Jeff) Harlin, was born January 23, 1871 and first attended the public school on Church Street between Main and Sycamore, later attending the high school located where the Y.M.C.A. is now* [205 West Civic Center Drive].
>
> *Lloyd Hill, son of Jasper Hill, was born December 18, 1870, according to his sister, Mrs. Margaret Everts of Long Beach, so the Hills appeared to have the best of the argument. Harlin's friends, however, claim that Tom was always a year ahead of Lloyd in school, and as Tom puts it, "It wasn't because I was so smart."*
>
> *Jeff Harlin had a general merchandise store in Santa Ana and owned the Harlin tract on East First Street.*
>
> *The mother of Lloyd Hill was Mrs. Maria Hill, daughter of Mr. and Mrs. Robert English and also a sister of Mrs. Jeanie Spurgeon* [William's wife], *who died here recently.*

An Early Grocery Store

Interviews with Waddy Johnson and Mr. Zelian shed some light on what grocery stories were like during Orange County's pioneer days, as well as the political hassles that sometimes accompanied the importing of goods to these stores.

> *How the children of the 60's and 70's loved the dark little grocery store with its odor of coffee and cheese and smoked meats!*
>
> *It was unlike a store of today. It was a one-room store with shelves behind a counter fourteen inches wide. If the storekeeper kept calico, he put it on one side of the store, and on the other side, the nails, chain, shovels, etc.*
>
> *The sugar barrel was in the center, and was covered with a mosquito netting fastened to a round whoop. In it was a scoop. With this the storekeeper measured out the sugar into packages of three and five pounds. He had no sacks and tied the sugar in brown paper. This was brown sugar,*

Two men stand in Richard Henry Seale's grocery store in Anaheim, circa 1880s. *Courtesy the Anaheim Public Library.*

made in New Orleans from sugar cane. It was sticky and very sweet and better for the body than the refined white sugar which did not come until 1890. The Indians and Mexicans were very fond of brown sugar, and on festivals, would buy a barrel of it, and put it on everything they ate.

The staple foods always found in stores were flour, bacon, crackers, and some cans of salmon.

The storekeeper was often a ruddy-faced German, bluff, but dear to the hearts of the boys. If he roared at them like an ogre in a fairy story, they were never afraid, for there was a merry twinkle in his eye. He often gave the children licorice or jelly beans, or sticks of red and white peppermint candy.

When Reinhaus Brothers first started in business, goods from the East would be shipped by boat to San Pedro, then they would have to have it hauled by oxen to Santa Ana, the roads being too bad to use horses. After the railroads were built, they would take the goods which arrived on the boats and hold them for three or five weeks before forwarding them out of San Pedro. They did this to spite the merchants who used the ships instead of shipping across the continent by rail.

When a truck company was started for the purpose of delivering the merchandise from the boats to the buyers, the railroads fought it and placed the matter into the hands of the State Railroad Commission. Reinhaus Brothers had records of the arrival of the boats and the time lapsed before the cargoes were forwarded by the railroads, and on this evidence the truck companies were allowed to handle the freight.

Mike Frankel operated a grocery and a dry goods store in competition with the Spurgeons but one day got into trouble with Ed Bush, who beat him up, and Frankel was afraid it wouldn't stop with the beating so sold out to Gildmacher who conducted the store for many years after.

Santa Ana's First Library

Mrs. Emma L. French moved to California from Boston around the end of 1870; by 1876, both she and her husband had moved to Santa Ana after becoming friendly with the Irvine family. Raising a young daughter in the fledgling city, Mrs. French quickly set out to form the city's first library.

Mr. French supplied a wardrobe for the books, and I was the librarian for two years. I drove from house to house, sometimes as far as the San Joaquin, collecting books, until the bottom of the buggy was full. Then the patrons met at the various homes and covered the books with paper to protect them.

Two flower festivals were given to raise funds for this library. Mr. Spurgeon donated his hall. Booths were assigned to various ladies, who sold flowers. Oysters, ice-cream, and sandwiches were for sale also. I took in thirty dollars in one night. Another way of raising money was to have various persons pose as statuary. A man with an oil-can would pretend to lubricate the joints of the statue while someone else would make a loud noise behind the statue, pretending that he was winding it up. Then suddenly the figure would move. If the statue was Jack-of-the-Bean-Stalk, gradually his knife would be thrust down to kill the woman kneeling at his feet.

Another time, when the statue would not move its arms, the operator cut off the arm to the horror of the assembled group. It was a wooden arm, and what fun it caused! We could raise a hundred dollars in a night.

Today, Santa Ana Public Library ranks among the one hundred largest libraries in the nation, housing almost 250,000 books. It is extremely fitting that the WPA volume that details Mrs. French's founding of the library is now housed in the very same institution.

Chapter 2
ANAHEIM

Anaheim's name comes from a combination of the Santa Ana River and the traditional German ending for place names, *heim*. One of the oldest settlements in Orange County, Anaheim's history is distinct from the surrounding communities such as Orange and Santa Ana. The city was founded in 1857 by a group of about fifty German immigrants—primarily winemakers. Although Orange County is no longer known for its wine production, these early German immigrants were responsible for creating the nucleus of what would one day grow into one of Southern California's most prominent cities.

German Immigrants to Anaheim

The WPA volume recounted the story of the movement of many German immigrants and additionally described some of the early colony's most prominent families.

> *The group of pioneers who located at the site of Anaheim in 1857 were for the most part natives of Germany. However, they did not emigrate directly from that county, but had previously taken up residence at San Francisco.*
>
> *During this period more than one half of the population of San Francisco were Germans. It may be well to state why there had been such*

an influx of Germans to America at that time. The German Empire at this time compelled all male citizens to enter the army and navy and serve for a number of years. To escape this service for themselves or their sons, they came in large numbers to the United States, many of them locating first at San Francisco.

To some extent, even to the present day [1936], *the German element of Anaheim retains not a little conservatism, and an expression of this is seen in the numerous churches, wherein, the German language is retained by their pastors in preaching the Christian doctrine. Many are the German gatherings held weekly of a social or educational nature, and the deportment of those participating always bespeaks the culture and enlightenment of the men, women, and children.*

The immigrants who came to California during the 50's were mostly political exiles, well-educated and persons of culture. Many of them were of the aristocracy and nobility, some of them locating in Anaheim. The occasion for these Germans coming to the Pacific Slope in the middle of the nineteenth century was their inherent love for adventure, their possessing

A view of West Center Street in Anaheim, circa 1873. On the left, a sign reads, "Dry Goods, Clothing." In the middle of the unpaved street, a man sits on a horse. The buildings seen in the photo were demolished shortly after the turn of the twentieth century. *Courtesy the Anaheim Public Library.*

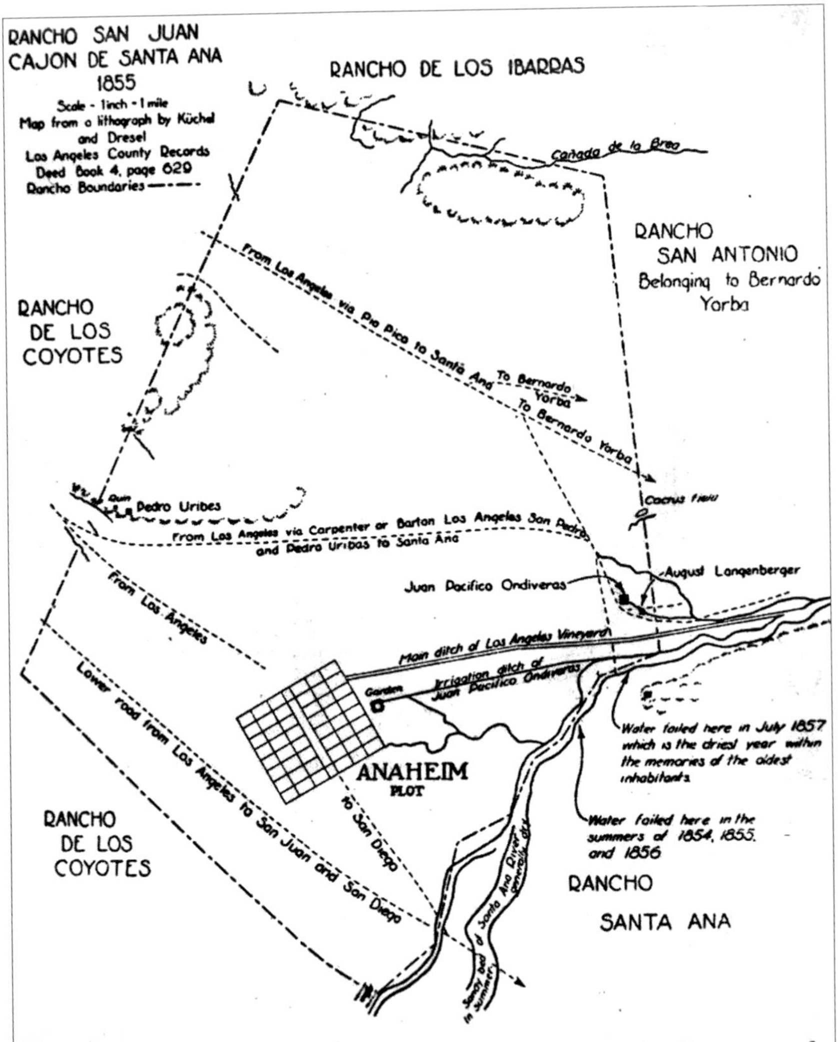

Fig. 2. Site of Anaheim, California, 1855. From Los Angeles County records.

An early map showing the location of Anaheim in relation to the Spanish ranchos that existed throughout Orange County at the time. Also marked are irrigation canals and stagecoach roads that provided crucial infrastructure to the city. *Courtesy the Anaheim Public Library.*

sufficient money for an extending journey, the reputed agreeable climate and opportunity to gain rich rewards from tilling the productive soil.

Those of the German immigrants who came west and to Anaheim were of a sturdy, hardworking nature, and the immense groves of citrus fruits and vegetable farms in and about Anaheim and throughout Orange County, at the present time, attest the successful endeavors of these early pioneers.

Among the early settlers of Anaheim, the name Dreyfus has been handed down as being that of a man who operated an extensive winery business. H. Kroeger was a progressive business man interested in many pursuits which benefitted Anaheim. G. Krouther was a blacksmith, a popular figure and respected citizen. A Mr. Conrad was a brewer with extensive holdings. Adolph Rimpau was proprietor of a jewelry store on Center Street. His store building was a conspicuous landmark for many years because of a sign in the form of a large rooster, made of metal, on the roof.

Another pioneer family that played a most important part in the settlement and development of Anaheim was the Yorba family. Without giving a detailed review of the history of the family mention should be made of them, because the entire city of Anaheim was once part and parcel of their property interests. Something like three hundred and sixty acres of the old Yorba estate still exists as a ranch within a few miles of the city of Anaheim. The Yorbas, whom history has often referred to, were not only progressive and thrifty, but they have always been prominent in their community, and have always been well-to-do. The names of Felipe Yorba, Prudencio Yorba, and Vicente Yorba are familiar to the older residents of Anaheim.

Perhaps one of the oldest and most rare antiques that exists in the State of California may be seen at the Yorba ranch near Anaheim. This consists of a large virgin copper kettle, hand-hammered and wrought. It is about four feet in diameter at the top and about three feet at the bottom. It flanges outward to a height of about eighteen inches. This kettle weighs about three hundred pounds. It was brought from Spain by Bernardo Yorba on his first trip here, and has remained a prized possession in his family ever since. It has a reputed age of two hundred years, and is surely a museum piece, and is well worth a trip to the ranch to see. [Although mentioned in many histories of the Yorba family, the current whereabouts of the kettle are unknown.]

Almost within a stone's throw of the ranch there was once in pioneer days a Catholic Church and a schoolhouse, and not far distant may still be seen the cemetery of the Yorba family, containing the remains of the pioneer members of this prominent clan.

The Yorba Cemetery was founded in 1858, and contains the remains of members of some of Orange County's most important early families. Since 1967 it has been administered by the County of Orange; at the time the WPA was writing, burials were still being held.

An early view of Los Angeles Street in Anaheim. Today, this street is Anaheim Boulevard. *Courtesy the Orange County Archives.*

The Dreyfus Winery was one of the first prominent businesses to call Anaheim home. While Central and Northern California are primarily known for their wine today, grapes were once grown in Orange County. Vineyards were also one of the most prosperous early developments in downtown Los Angeles. *Courtesy the Anaheim Public Library.*

Business Street in Anaheim, 1880s. Numerous horse-drawn carriages fill the street, which is lined on either side by some of Anaheim's earliest businesses. Due to widespread development over the decades, there is no trace of any commercial structures from this era. *Courtesy the Anaheim Public Library.*

As is well known the early settlers of Anaheim were colonists from San Francisco and were mostly Germans. After their arrival here they communicated with their relatives in the Fatherland, explaining the many opportunities this land offered for material advancement. This persuaded quite a number of German emigrants to take up residence here. The pioneer population consisted of about fifty families, numbering about four hundred persons.

Many of the early settlers and those who came thereafter were of a hard working class and brought many articles with them to assist them in gaining a livelihood. Carpenter tools, agricultural implements, household furnishings, quaint, old-fashioned pictures, and many other things dear to their hearts were brought by these sturdy Germans to the land of promise.

It is not uncommon to see many of these articles in the homes of the descendants of these pioneers. Many homes in Anaheim are now adorned with these old-time pictures in their curious frames, and are treasured by their owners, who proudly show them to visitors.

German Customs in Early Anaheim

WPA writers documented some of the customs in Anaheim that early settlers brought over from Germany. In their dress and celebrations, Anaheim's pioneers maintained a remarkable degree of cultural integrity.

> *It is interesting to note the type of dress worn by the early settlers of Anaheim. The women dressed with about the same number of garments. The garments were often bright and gay and as many of them came from the southern part of Germany they retained with their style and cut. The women wore full, heavy cloth skirts with a short jacket worn over a shirt waist of plain material without decoration. Stockings were knit of heavy wool yarn of different colors. Shoes were of heavy calfskin, either with buttons or laced, with pointed toes which turned slightly upward. The headdress of these early pioneer women consisted either of a shawl or curiously shaped little bonnet. A few of them went bareheaded.*
>
> *In a few instances these people brought with them crudely shaped slippers made of wood that were known as sabots. These were rarely worn on the streets but were worn during household duties. Many of these wooden shoes are still in the possession of the descendants of*

Both the Planters and Anaheim Hotels are seen in this early aerial view, along with the locations of the city's several fraternal organizations and churches. Anaheim could boast a daily newspaper as early as the time this lithograph was made. *Courtesy the University of California.*

the pioneers. They are treasured for their sentiment rather than for any usefulness they may now possess.

The children of the pioneers and those who came later were immediately placed in school that they might acquire the English language. The dress of the little boys was much as it is today. The little girls, however, were more conspicuous with their bright colored dresses, displaying ribbons and many buttons. The dresses were cut high at the waist, with a rather full skirt reaching much below the knees, giving the girls the appearance of being much older than they really were.

In some of the schools the German language was taught, but the attendance was not to be compared in numbers with those schools teaching elementary English. Their attendance at school was punctual and constant, and they readily adapted themselves to the change in education from which many of them had formerly been accustomed.

In all Christendom, the holiday of Christmas is the most important holiday of the year. So also was it with the early founders of Anaheim. Catholics and Protestants alike were wont to celebrate the day as a whole. The Catholics who came here from Northern Germany were accustomed to having their tables spread for a feast, and lights burning during the entire night, that the Virgin Mary and the angel who passes when everyone is asleep may find something to eat.

The decorations of the German household began as early as the morning of the 24th of December. One room, from which all but "die Mutter" [the mother] *was excluded, contained the Christmas tree, with all the presents set in a shining row upon the table. Greens were hung from the windows and doors and garlands upon the walls. Upon the dining room table a great cold supper was spread. Family and guests began to gather at five o'clock. The children's eyes were glued to the main entrance, which presently swung open and revealed the tree. Six o'clock—all doors were swung open, revealing the rooms resplendent with lights and tinsel.*

The children were often restrained with difficulty from pouncing upon the tree while the presents were being taken from the branches and distributed. Everyone kissed and for two or three hours the labors of the field or household were forgotten. A late supper and then to bed. Christmas day was spent exchanging presents and receiving and paying calls. The evening was given over to dancing, with music and much merriment.

The festival of Kermiss was and still is popular in parts of Germany, Belgium, and Holland. In Southern Germany it is known as Kirchweithe, or church consecration. Kermiss is given over to a day of rejoicing, an out and out German holiday. The festivities are usually held in some park where all kinds of games, including races and matches of strength are enjoyed.

During the year 1883, Anaheim celebrated such a day. The affair was attended by the majority of the inhabitants of the town, who planned the

One of Anaheim's multiple livery stables, Fashion Stables, can be seen in this 1887 photograph. With the coming of the railroad (and, subsequently, automobiles), livery stables were one of the first industries to disappear. *Courtesy the Los Angeles Public Library.*

Another view of Anaheim's Fashion Stables, this time seen with a horse-drawn streetcar parked in front. Numerous streetcar lines ran throughout the county during its pioneer days. *Courtesy the Anaheim Public Library.*

festivities, picnicking in a grove in the western part of Anaheim. As years passed by, however, the Kermiss in Anaheim gradually lost its religious character, and sometimes even gave rise to brawls and other excesses. Beer and ale, brewed locally was the favorite drink, and there seemed to have been plenty for all, gratis.

The day was usually celebrated in Anaheim, as in Germany, in the fall, the latter part of September, or the first part of October. There seems to have been so many and various acts and incident that took place during the Kermiss that the more one becomes acquainted with the festivity the more exhaustive becomes the subject. Many of the present day residents of Anaheim tell of their presence at these occasions, which are not held as frequently as in former years.

Still another pretty German custom seems to have been in favor in the Fatherland, and for a time after the settling of Anaheim was in favor here. This was the gathering of the people on St. Andrew's Day, November 30. To learn which persons at the gathering love each other and will one day be united, a vessel of pure water is placed upon a table. Little cups of tinfoil, inscribed with the names of those having their fortunes told, are set afloat upon the water in the vessel. If a youth's cup advances towards the cup of a maiden, he will make the first advances, but if the maiden's cup advances toward that of the youth's, she will make the first advances. Should the cups meet, they will be sweethearts. Still other cups are set floating marked as priests, and it is only when the youth and maiden coming together get a priest between them, that they may expect to get married.

Anaheim Polish Colony

Perhaps Orange County's first resident celebrity was Helena Modjeska, one of the most famous Shakespearean actresses of the twentieth century. Although her story has been told numerous times, most notably in her autobiography, *Memories and Impressions*, the WPA's account of her life both in Poland and California is worth retelling for its brevity and amusing anecdotes.

The Brook Farm Experiment in New England, which was made up of a group of artists and writers who planned to live together as a small unit of society, is familiar to many, but perhaps few are aware that in our own Orange County there once existed a similar experiment. Its importance lies not in its numbers, but in the fact that it included the distinguished actress,

The Planters Hotel, located on the northwest corner of Lincoln Avenue and Anaheim Boulevard, was one of Anaheim's most prominent early establishments. The building burned to the ground in 1890. *Courtesy the Los Angeles Public Library.*

Madame Helena Modjeska, who was afterwards to establish a home in this county.

The idea had its beginnings one winter evening back in 1875 when a company of friends were gathered in Modjeska's home in Warsaw. In the group was the distinguished Polish writer Henryk Sienkiewicz. Conversation turned to the Centennial Exposition which was about to be held in Philadelphia and Sienkiewicz in his characteristic manner, described California in most glowing terms. In her "Memories," Modjeska gives some amusing opinions expressed by members of the group concerning the Golden West.

"You cannot die of hunger," said one. "Rabbits, hares, and partridges are unguarded. You have only to go out and shoot them."

"Coffee grows wild. All you have to do is pick it," said another. "And gold—they say, you can dig it out almost anywhere."

While the discussion was at its height, the family doctor entered and jokingly said to Modjeska, "You need a change of air, Madame. Why not make a trip to America?" Count Chlapowski, Modjeska's husband, thought the idea a good one, and someone else immediately exclaimed, "Let us all go. We will kill pumas, build huts, make our own garments out of skins and live as our forefathers lived." However, at the time the subject was dismissed as an impossibility.

Not long afterward, Modjeska's fourteen year old son Rudolphe, who had decided to become an engineer, became very anxious to visit the Exposition and then cross Panama to California. Modjeska was in poor health, so her husband urged the trip in the hope that it would prove beneficial to her. Friends of the family became interested in the new county and a few of them felt that it would be delightful to live where there could be no oppression such as existed in Russia or Prussian Poland. Henryk Sienkiewicz was among the first to suggest the emigration, and soon five others expressed a wish to seek adventure.

So seriously was the idea considered that the group secured a teacher of English and started to prepare themselves for life in the new country. They even wrote rules by with they were to be governed. The new land was looked upon as a sort of Utopia where conditions would be ideal.

Modjeska obtained a leave of absence for one year, fully expecting to return even before that time. In the early spring of 1876, Henryk Sienkiewicz and Julian Sypniewski sailed for the new world. It was planned for the others to follow in July. Sypniewski returned with glowing accounts of the beauty of California. He described it as a paradise indeed, and no wonder, for it was early spring just following heavy rains when everything looked green. Sienkiewicz also wrote convincing letters. Extensive preparations were made for the journey. Many things were bought including medicine boxes, a large array of surgical instruments, and a half-dozen revolvers. Books and pictures were carefully packed as they were regarded as quite essential for this "simple life" in the wilderness.

After a most impressive farewell performance, Modjeska and her party left for America. In the group were her husband and son, Rudolphe, Julian Sypniewski, his wife and two children, L. Paprocki, a cartoonist, and Anusia, a sixteen-year-old girl who had been engaged to take care of the children, and whom Modjeska expected to train for a housemaid on the community farm.

The ocean voyage proved a most delightful experience for Modjeska, for she was fascinated by the sea. In fact all of the party seemed happy except Mrs. Sypniewski, who according to Modjeska, "drooped like a water lily."

After a stay in the East, the party came to San Francisco via Panama. Modjeska and her husband stayed in the city a short time in order that they might see the great actor Edwin Booth who was playing there, while the rest of the party went south to Anaheim. This town had been decided upon by Mr. Sypniewski as appropriate for the colony because of the German families he had met there during his previous voyage. He thought that it would be easier to begin ranch life among people with whom they could talk, as the Polish group spoke little German, but were as not yet able to grasp English.

The house that had been rented proved rather small for there were only two bedrooms, a dining room, and a so-called parlor. It certainly presented an unpromising appearance with its shaggy grass, its cypresses and a few flowers scattered at random, and looking as Modjeska said like a poorly kept graveyard. But it had one redeeming feature—the view of the mountains of the Sierra Madre to the north, and the Santa Ana Range on the east. Because of the cramped quarters of the house, an old barn standing near the house was arranged as sleeping quarters for Sienkiewicz and Paprocki.

The first day's work on the ranch was started with enthusiasm. At the end of the day the workers returned tired, but still hopeful. The fifteen-year-old son of the family, who was working with the men, even played one of Chopin's waltzes to see whether his fingers had been made stiff from the hoe, and Sienkiewicz read one of his "Charcoal Sketches." Next morning some were late to breakfast, the third day someone had a lame back, and by the end of the week, Modjeska's husband and son were the only ones who were working. Everyone else it seemed had an excuse to be doing something else. Sienkiewicz had a letter to write, Paprocki, unable to walk from rheumatism was making drawings, while Sypniewski found it necessary to look after his wife. Sypniewski was the only one of the group who possessed any agricultural knowledge, but it could not be applied very satisfactorily to a new soil and climate. It was a group of idealists who worked when they felt like it, discussed a great deal, sometimes quarreled, and in short lived under a nervous tension that could not be conductive to the success of the undertaking.

Horseback riding was a favorite recreation of the group. They had several saddle horses which were named after the well-known characters in Poland. All the horses except the buggy team were broncos, and were often quite vicious, but their riders did not seem to mind, and enjoyed galloping over the cactus and sagebrush frightening away the squirrels, rabbits and quail. Hunting was a favorite past time, so there was usually plenty of rabbits and quail to eat, and occasionally wild ducks or geese. The maid Anusia dressed the birds, and used the wings lavishly for decorating her hat, having as many as seventeen wings pinned to it at one time.

As weeks passed the little colony grew more and more restless and despondent and desperately homesick. One afternoon when they were feeling unusually downcast, they were visited by Mr. J.E. Pleasants, and his Spanish wife Dona Refugia. The visit proved a very pleasant one, the conversation being carried on in broken English and broken Spanish. The Pleasants extended an invitation to the colonists to visit them in their homestead in the Santa Ana Mountains.

Not long afterwards it was decided to take a vacation from farming and visit some of the neighboring places. The first trip was an excursion to Anaheim Landing, and Modjeska gives an amusing description of it. All of the party, including the maid went on the trip, the women and children in a buggy and the men on horseback. That they did not lack attention one can easily guess, and no doubt created as much interest as Hollywood movie actors on location. They met many interesting people—Spaniards and cowboys including the "Senora Coyote," driving her half-starved horse. The nickname had been given to the old lady by Indians who worked in her vineyard. She had come originally from northern Europe and was one of the earliest settlers in Anaheim. She had a reputation for rigid economy and could not bear to waste anything. One day when a coyote was killed and brought to her she did not even thank the one who had killed it, but later she skinned the animal and cooked the meat for the dinner of the Indian workmen. A little boy who had seen her doing it reported the incident, so it won for her the name of "Senora Coyote."

On this trip to Anaheim Landing, Sienkiewicz showed the party the interesting spots, and the shanty where he wrote his stories.

The site of the ocean made Modjeska so homesick that she was in despair for days after the trip to Anaheim Landing. She seemed indifferent to everything, until a short time later when the party made an excursion to the Santiago Canyon in the Santa Ana Mountains where the Pleasants lived. On the way they stopped at Orange County Park [now Hart Park in Orange] *whose fine old live oaks overhung with grapevines and other attractions made a strong appeal. Mr. and Mrs. Pleasants were away, but the party had an opportunity to admire the surroundings. There was an arbor covered with vines and roses on the outside and fitted up on the inside with rustic furniture for a living room and dining room. A stove under an oak tree served as a kitchen. Pantry shelves were conveniently built into the cavity of the same tree. Wild lilac, honeysuckle, and oaks with a mountain in the foreground made it a picturesque spot indeed. To Modjeska, it looked more like fantastic stage scenery than the real thing, and reminded her strongly of her stage days. No doubt it was the interest aroused in this beauty spa on this day that a few years later prompted Modjeska to buy this place which she named the "Forest of Arden."*

When the party return to Anaheim there was a letter awaiting them from Captain P. of San Francisco announcing his intention of visiting them. Preparations for the guest at once began. The sofa in the parlor was replaced by a bed, while the son, Rudolphe, joined the two men in the barn. The most important question was the menu, for the captain had a colossal appetite in keeping with his great size. For the first dinner it was decided to have a turkey—but who was to kill it? Nobody was eager for the job, finally after a consultation, a hatchet was secured, and operations began. Count Chlapowski held the legs, Paprocki the head while Sienkiewicz acted as executioner.

When the captain arrived the next morning he succeeded in dispelling all the gloom that had been hanging over the household. Modjeska says that he seemed suited to the seventeenth century rather than to a modern era and for humor might be compared to Sir Toby Belch [*Twelfth Night*] *or Falstaff* [*Henry IV*].

Perhaps the visit of the captain had greater significance than merely a pleasant interlude for those he was visiting, for Modjeska thinks it quite likely that it was the captain whom Sienkiewicz had in mind when he created the character of Zagloba in his historical trilogy of "Fire and Sword," "Deluge," *and* "Pan Michal."

A period of gloom seemed to follow the captain's departure. It was November and the weather grew cloudy and windy and seemed to depress

Shakespearean actress Helena Modjeska poses in front of her home, Arden, where she lived from 1888 to 1906. The area is still known as Modjeska Canyon today. *Courtesy the Los Angeles Public Library.*

Another view of Modjeska's Arden, which operates as a museum and historic site today. *Courtesy the Los Angeles Public Library.*

everybody. On one of these days the little company fell to comparing their anticipations of ideal life in California with its realities, and came to the conclusion that their farming experiment was not a success. There were cows but nobody to milk them, so they had to buy milk, butter, and cream from their neighbors. The dogs ate the eggs, the grapes were not marketed, and the neighbors' cattle ate the barley. Fifteen thousand dollars had been spent in the undertaking and Modjeska was unwilling that her husband should continue to finance it. She decided to go to San Francisco and study English in preparation for the stage. For a time her husband and son remained on the farm, for they wished to sell it. Some time later, together with Paprocki, they spent some time on a claim in the Santiago Canyon near the Pleasants' home. It was a rather primitive life here, for the house was only a shack, and wild game was plentiful. Rattlesnake, grizzlies, and even mountain lions were not uncommon.

Modjeska's son soon joined her in San Francisco, but it was necessary for her husband to remain in or near Anaheim for a time as it was found that it was harder to sell a farm than to buy one. Sienkiewicz had already left for the north, and Count Chlapowski felt a responsibility for Sypniewski

> *whom he brought to this country. Eventually, he did send him and his family back to Poland.*
>
> *That this farming experiment should fail was inevitable from the beginning, but perhaps it had its justification in giving to America a great actress. Modjeska says that it was her intention to return to the stage after her health had been restored, but she might not if life on the Anaheim farm had proved as attractive as the little group of colonists had hoped. From the early eighties until the close of the century she lived the life of an artist and was known to the theatre goers of two continents as no other of her time except* [Sarah] *Bernhardt.*
>
> *In 1902 Modjeska withdrew from the stage and settled in her mountain home in the Santiago Canyon about twenty miles from Santa Ana. The home, designed by the famous architect Stanford White, was in harmony with the scenic beauty of the surroundings. As many of the natural features were preserved as possible, including the oaks and wild shrubs. It was an ideal place to rest and for a year and a half Modjeska enjoyed the quiet beauty of her beloved "Arden" with no thought of returning to the stage. Then Paderewski came for a visit and while there persuaded her to again make a tour of the United States.*
>
> *Although the tour was to have been a short one, it was prolonged until 1907. When Modjeska returned to California the ranch in the canyon had been sold as it was too expensive to maintain. Because of her desire to be near the sea, Modjeska settled in Newport where she died April 8, 1909. Her remains were taken to her native home in Krakow, Poland, for burial.*

Today, Madame Modjeska's home is open to visitors as a museum, and the entire canyon where Arden is located has been named Modjeska Canyon in her honor. The Modjeska House is considered by many to be one of the most important historical landmarks in Orange County. A statue of Helena Modjeska was also created by the New Deal's Public Works of Art Project in 1934; it still stands in Anaheim's Pearson Park, not far from the site of Modjeska's failed attempt at a farm.

Chapter 3

ANAHEIM LANDING

One of Orange County's long-forgotten communities is Anaheim Landing, located on the eastern end of what is now Seal Beach. Shortly after the community of Anaheim was founded in 1857, locals founded the seaport of Anaheim Landing to handle commerce to and from the inland settlement. Although treacherous to ships, Anaheim Landing was a fairly successful port and predated both Long Beach and Newport Beach.

Once the shipping business was taken over by other safer and more developed ports, Anaheim Landing continued to exist as a seaside resort for people from the central part of the county. Anaheim Landing became known to locals as Bay City, and development during the first decades of the twentieth century moved the settlement to the current location of Seal Beach. Once Seal Beach was incorporated in 1915 and became a permanent city, Anaheim Landing shrank rapidly. Within a few decades, no trace of the former settlement was left. Today, a plaque at the corner of Seal Beach Boulevard and Electric Avenue is the only reminder of the community that once occupied the site.

Reminisces About Anaheim Landing

Mrs. Frank Groom, formerly Mrs. William White, was one of Anaheim's pioneers during the early 1880s and had many memories of traveling to Anaheim Landing.

A row of shacks line the beach at Anaheim Landing. Although no trace of the community exists today, the landing allowed for the fledgling community of Anaheim to prosper, when so many other settlements founded at that time have since disappeared. *Courtesy the Los Angeles Public Library.*

It was about '81 or '82 when my former husband, William White, and I came with our little girl, Cora, to Anaheim from Kansas. We rented a house from "Mother" Robinson near where she lived, quite close to the corner of Palm Street and Broadway, Anaheim.

Mrs. Robinson was a widow at the time we came. Before her husband's death, she and Mr. Robinson conducted a school for Indians in the long building where she lived. There were two Robinson girls, one of them named Florie. I cannot recall the name of the other one.

I speak of the Robinsons because they were frequently at Anaheim Landing and the girls were both wonderful swimmers. In fact, I should say they were the best swimmers in this section of the county at that time. They were both large, light-complexioned girls—very jolly.

When we came my husband was in such poor health that the doctors recommended sea bathing, thinking that might build him up physically. It was our custom therefore to spend a great deal of time camping at Anaheim Landing, it being the closest beach. It was really quite a lively place in those days and was the scene of most of the holiday celebration.

In those days, roads did not exist between Anaheim and the Landing, as Mrs. Groom recalls in this humorous anecdote about how she met her second husband:

> *People drove there over salt-grass pasture land just about making their own road as they went. The distance from Anaheim was twelve miles. On one occasion I remember that I drove my long-legged bay mare, Dolly, to Anaheim from our camp and I'm landing to get the mail and some provisions and on the return trip I noticed a man and a boy in a cart clipping it off at a lively pace towards the Landing. They were driving a small grey that was certainly a stepper. I was angling across the pasture near a gate and they evidently saw me for they pulled up and the boy got out and opened the gate. My mare had longer legs than their horse but she was tired and they had a cart and mine was a top buggy. Nothing was said about the race, of course, but when two good horses met that was usually what happened and that is what did happen that day. I beat them into the Landing. The boy in that cart was Frank Groom and with him was his older half-brother F.C. Bradley, who lives now at third and Bristol Street in Santa Ana. I didn't know them then.*

When Mrs. Groom got to this point in the interview, Mr. Groom had the following to add.

> *Mr. Groom spoke up and said he remembered the incident but that the reason they didn't win the race was that some men that they knew stopped them and wanted them to have a drink and even though they didn't indulge in the refreshment, the delay caused them to lose the race. Another thing that marks the day for him was that it was the first day he ever smoked cigarettes and his brother lectured him about it almost all the way. Groom was fifteen years old at the time. The M.A. Groom family lived four and one-half miles south of Garden Grove on Orana Road which used to be called Garden Grove Road then. The family came from Missouri in 1875.*

After her husband's clarification about the race, Mrs. Groom resumed her reminiscing.

> *I remember one day that we were at the Landing and someone dared the Robinson girls to take the small rowboat that was tied to the pier in front of the warehouse and row out to the lighthouse that was out in the ocean a*

little south of the opening of the bay, climb to the top of the lighthouse and dive off. We saw them climb to the top and dive off and swim all around and then they got into the boat and returned.

One night we watched a large steamer anchor out from the Landing. It was all lit up. And the men from the warehouse worked some time going back and forth in small boats bringing in the merchandise. It was quite a sight. They stored the things in the warehouse to be distributed later. The warehouse, I would say, was about 40 feet by 60 feet in size.

About 49 years ago, the Malvern Hill Post, Grand Army of the Republic, of Anaheim, had its convention at Anaheim Landing. The Anaheim band played, and people came for many miles to the celebration. Mr. William Hounsom was the president of the Post and my husband, Mr. White, was vice-president. We were having such a good time when, along in the afternoon, the news spread through the crowd that the fourteen-year-old daughter of one of the merry-makers had drowned in Alamitos Bay [now part of Long Beach]. *It seems that the children had gone to pick wild flowers and had wandered as far as Alamitos Bay. There they decided to wade and the girl lost her footing. The other children couldn't swim and when they saw what was happening they rushed away in terror for assistance. I was frantic because I couldn't find my own little girl and I learned that she had gone with the other children. At last, I found her and she was carrying her grey kitty. It seems that the cat had followed the children and they didn't see it until they had gone some distance, so my girl, Cora, picked the cat up and took it with her rather than bring it back. It may be that the cat's aversion to the water of Alamitos Bay kept my child from harm that day. At any rate she was safe but frightened when I found her.*

When they brought the body of the drowned child they carried her into the warehouse. They worked for some time trying to revive her but she was too far gone. I remember that they laid her on one of the beds near and just inside the warehouse door. It was the custom in those days for each family to rope off sleeping quarters within the warehouse. Mr. Backs, who was in the undertaking business in Anaheim, came and took charge of the body. Of course, we were all so saddened by the tragedy that we packed up and left. I cannot recall the name of the child that was drowned; it seems to me that her first name was Viola. The family name may have been Wagner or Matthews. It was so long ago that I just cannot remember. They lived near the Tuffrey family in Anaheim.

Horses are seen roaming free in the small community of Anaheim Landing. Located between Seal Beach and Surfside, there is now only a plaque commemorating the former settlement. *Courtesy the Anaheim Public Library.*

Mrs. Groom continued by reflecting on what happened after the Landing's heyday, when many residents had moved away or passed on.

> *I understand that "Florie" Robinson, whom I have already mentioned, is dead now. The other Robinson girl went to San Francisco to teach and I heard that she married a doctor of that city. Both of the girls were teachers.*
>
> *After my husband, Mr. White, died in Anaheim and the removal of Mr. and Mrs. Hounsom to Los Angeles, the charter for the Malvern Hill Post, G.A.R., was surrendered.*

She concluded with one last humorous story about what life was like when the Landing was the region's sole seaside town.

> *At the time I came to Anaheim there was no Long Beach. We used to drive to Los Angeles by way of Bixby Hill, on over the hill to a eucalyptus grove, then turn north. I remember one occasion when we drove our surrey and Mr. and Mrs. Hounsom drove theirs over this route to Los Angeles to see a parade. It was a warm day and the road was lined on both sides with mustard as high as the horses' backs. The horses were bitten by flies all the way, even though we had them covered with nets. You may be sure that we didn't appreciate the many carriages decorated with mustard in the parade that day.*

Fortification of Anaheim Landing

The other passage about Anaheim Landing in the WPA's volume revolves around a very different subject. Five men and women who spent time at Anaheim Landing were interviewed regarding the existence of fortifications left over from the Mexican-American War.

Philip A. Stanton, Former State Senator

A short distance back of the bay there was a ridge or hill which had an elevation of 48 feet and extended the entire width of the distance between the two inlets or bays. Mr. Stanton noticed what appeared to be an old irrigation ditch on the north side, or the side facing away from the ocean. As the ground was so damp that it had to be drained before it could be farmed and water for domestic use could be obtained anywhere by driving a piece of iron pipe down a few feet, he was at a loss to understand why a long, deep ditch should have been dug at that spot.

Making inquiries from the people who had lived on the property for some time, he was told that the ditch had been dug by the American soldiers during the Mexican War as defense for Anaheim Landing.

As the ranch was used for raising cattle and sheep for many years the trench was partially filled in by constant tramping down. At the time of the World War it was put into cultivation and all traces of the trench were destroyed in leveling off the land.

Harry Anderson

Harry Anderson, whose parents were the first couple to locate in Westminster after it had been founded in 1875, still lives on the original ranch bought by his parents. He has been familiar with Anaheim Landing all of his life and remembers the trench on the side of the hill facing the bay and says it was common knowledge in the early days that the trench had been built by the American forces to protect the Landing. Mr. Anderson says that after the shipping had ceased at Anaheim Landing, the large warehouse was partitioned off by Mr. Michael of Redlands, and rented to people who came to the Bay for vacations, until it was destroyed by fire about 1904.

Ed Larter

Ed Larter came to Westminster in 1875, he was fond of shooting and hunting around Anaheim Landing and Los Alamitos Bay on many occasions. He was familiar with the entire country around the bays and remembers the ditch on the side of the hill which he was told had been a trench built by the American soldiers during the war with Mexico. It was about three quarters of a mile long, extended the entire distance between the two bays. All the dirt had been thrown on the upper side of the trench so that it was evident that soldiers stationed in the trench could shoot any one the moment they appeared coming over the hill and before they could advance far enough to shoot down at the men in the trench. In other words, the soldiers landing at the bay would have to cross the trench before coming inland, and as soon as their heads showed above the crest of the hill they could be shot by the soldiers in the trench stationed a few feet below them. Mr. Larter states that the thousands of sheep and cattle pastured there for years gradually leveled it off and that the farmers obliterated all traces of the trench when they began raising crops on the hill at the time of the World War.

Judge Ord

Judge Ord of Seal Beach also recalls this trench and says that they used fresnos (a wide scoop scraper) to fill it in. That it also seemed poor military strategy to have the trench so far back from the ocean.

Mrs. Martha Wardlow

Martha E. Wardlow, Santa Ana, came to California with her two brothers from Burlington, Kansas, in 1875, and located at Downey. She and her husband Robert B. Wardlow removed to the Bixby Ranch about 1878.

Mrs. Wardlow says that many of the squatters on the Stearns Ranch bought land and located on the Bixby Ranch after they had been evicted from the Stearns property.

She remembers the trench on the Bixby Hill which she was told had been thrown up by the American forces during the Mexican War but thinks it had been leveled off and all traces of it destroyed.

The thought of Mexican-American War fortifications existing in Orange County may seem incredible at first, but given the large presence of troops in San Pedro, it is by no means implausible. Whether there was ever any fighting seen in the county remains a mystery (realistically, there probably wasn't), but the brief recollections of some of the county's pioneers are a tantalizing glimpse into an even more distant period of the area's history.

Chapter 4

ORANGE

The city of Orange was founded by two men whose names will be familiar to anyone who visits the city's downtown: Alfred Chapman and Andrew Glassell. Prominent attorneys from Los Angeles, they selected the site of Orange due to its prime agricultural conditions. Development of the town began to increase during the early 1870s, when the first school, grocery store and post office opened.

Although the county is now famous for its prodigious orange crops, most early pioneers relied on crops such as barley, rye, wheat, corn and oats. As with Anaheim, grapes were also an important crop early on. Less successful were tropical fruits such as pineapples and guavas.

The stories about Orange in the WPA's *Pioneer Tales* paint the picture of a quiet, agricultural town that was still deeply entrenched in its Mexican heritage. The landscape painted by many of the stories is nothing short of idyllic.

Old Days in Richland

Orange was originally named Richland, but in 1873, it was discovered that there was already a town in northern California with that same name. Richland's residents quickly proposed the alternate name of "Orange," which stuck and is still in use more than 140 years later. Here, a pioneer woman named Jennie Hayward Parker tells stories about what the city was like around the time of the name change.

> *Perhaps the best way to tell the early history of Orange is to give the story of the lady, who came to Orange in 1873, Mrs. Jennie Hayward Parker, who passed away several years ago.*
>
> *De Witt Hayward came from Iowa in 1871 for rheumatism, a disease from which he had suffered since he was four years old. He was completely cured.*

Andrew Glassell (1827–1901), a wealthy real estate attorney and investor, was one of the founders of the city of Orange. Glassell Street is still named in his honor. *Courtesy University of Southern California.*

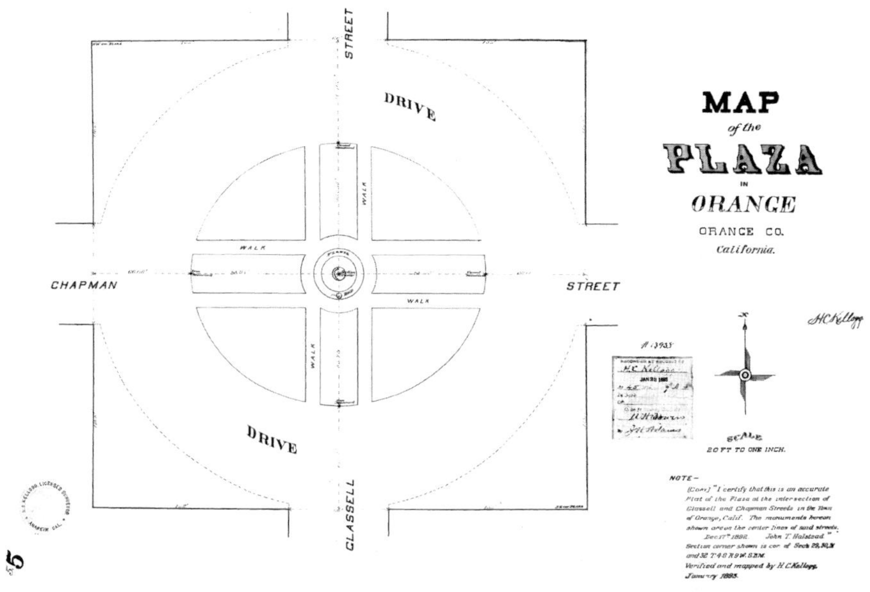

An early map of the Orange Plaza from January 1895. The Plaza, which dates to the city of Orange's earliest days, is one of the few features from pioneer Orange County that has persisted into modern times. *Courtesy the Orange County Archives.*

A little later De Witt's mother came for a visit and De Witt accompanied her home. As De Witt did not care to return alone he persuaded his sister Jennie to come with him. They came by train to San Francisco, and then a three-days' journey by sea on the old Mahonga, a side-wheeler, which later was destroyed, brought them to Wilmington. They were met by some friends, who drove them in a spring wagon, and brought them to Orange in December, 1873.

They found only a few houses in the town and a small ranch population scattered through the vicinity of Orange as it now stands. There were no business places in Orange, and the people went to Anaheim for their mail. There was a general merchandise store in Santa Ana owned by Mr. Spurgeon, where the Spurgeon block now stands. He had an artesian well back of the store, and the hitching-racks for the horses.

There were good stores in Anaheim, and the business was divided between the two places. An early bitterness between Orange and Santa Ana over water divisions, ditches and the like, caused some Orange folks to leave out Santa Ana altogether as a trading place, but these were few.

The first store in Orange was built by the Fisher boys, and about '76 or '77 it became the Grange Store with J. W. Anderson as the proprietor. The store was remodeled and had an upstairs added, and there the Grange meetings were

A circa 1890 aerial view of the Orange Plaza shows how little development there was in the city when the tract of land was laid out. The Plaza'a original fountain was replaced during the 1930s; more recently, it was refurbished and now sits outside Orange's city hall. *Courtesy the Orange Public Library.*

held, and there many of the good times of the day centered. Millard Parker, son of Joshua D. Parker, who became the husband of Jennie Hayward, owned the drug store opposite the Grange store just north of Chapman Avenue. The Grange was on the northwest corner of the Plaza and the drugstore on the northeast. Mr. Parker lived only a few years.

When Mrs. Parker arrived in Orange there was but one orange tree in all the country round. Mr. A.B. Chapman of the Chapman and Glassell firm had an office in what is now the Plaza Square, and in front of the office there was a large orange tree which he had transplanted full-size, bringing it from Los Angeles.

Joshua Parker had come from San Jose with his big boys and bought a ranch at the corner of Main and Chapman, and wanted to try out the orange business. He drove to Los Angeles in a lumber wagon and bought six trees at ten dollars a piece. People were getting interested! In her husband's diary Mrs. Parker finds a note where twelve orange seeds had been taken from an orange and planted. D.C. Hayward bought thirty acres at Palmyra and Glassell and begin the nursery business. He sent to Florida and oranges were sent to him in barrels. By the time they arrived the fruit was quite rotten. It was Mrs. Parker's job, by way of making some spending money to extract the seeds from the Florida oranges. It was not a very pleasant task. And thus was ushered in the beginning of the great orange industry. Mr. Hayward secured an expert budder, who put two pieces of buds together and quickly developed a small orange tree, which looked very handsome in the tub. Mr. Hayward took a good many of these trees with the fruit to San Francisco, where he sold them at a good price. He explained to the people that they would not live long in that northern climate, but they were beautiful and they sold.

In 1874 Rev. Samuel Bland, Presiding Elder of this district for the M.E. Church, came to Orange to start a church. The people of the community were promised a community center and gave liberally, but when the church was erected Mr. Bland said that it could not be a community church. They could have a Sabbath School, if they wished, but if they had a church, it must be Methodist, and it couldn't be anything else. This produced quite a row, but it became a Methodist Church where all came to worship together for a year or two. Then the Presbyterian brethren, begin holding services in the afternoon in the M.E. Church. This had been promised them when "the row" was settled and when the Presbyterians became strong enough for a group of their own, the use of the building was to be theirs and welcome. But it was only a short time when they were asked to pay rent. This so stirred their righteous souls that they held Sabbath School and church in the schoolhouse. In Westminster there were six Presbyterian ministers, one of whom was a young man by the name of Robert Strong. He passed away some years ago in Pasadena. Robert McPherson had lived in Westminster a short time before coming to Orange. One day when he was talking with Robert Strong, he said: "The Presbyterians of Orange wish to have services of their own." So Robert Strong came and preached for them for a time. But when their church life became a settled fact, they called Rev. Alles, who was the first regular pastor. Mr. Stephen McPherson rode around on horseback and learned how many Presbyterians there were and whether they wished to build a church. The movement for a church of their own was soon on foot. They found seventeen Presbyterians, but by the time they were ready to dedicate the church, one had married a Methodist and there were only sixteen. The early ministers were Rev. Alles, P.D. Young, Halliday, and in 1883 Rev. A. Parker, which is a later date by far than this short paper covers.

Rev. Young owned an orange orchard on east Walnut Avenue and took a practical and helpful interest in all that pertained to the welfare of the growing community.

Rev. William Knighten was the first minister of the Methodist Church. For many years he was a prominent minister of the Methodist Church in Southern California.

A view of a horse-drawn carriage on Chapman Street between Orange and the now defunct town of McPherson. *Courtesy the Orange Public Library.*

The school was started in 1873. Five acres were purchased where the Lemon Street school now stands between Olive and Glassell. It was a one-room building, 18x18 feet, and Mr. Stephen McPherson was the first teacher. It remained a one-room school for several years, when another room was added.

For three years there has been a most disastrous drought, disastrous especially to the hopes and visions of this little group of pioneers of Richland for so the little town was called at that time. And then in '74 came a terrible downpour. It rained seven days without stopping, was cloudy a day or two, and then rained two days. Our Santa Ana River went on a rampage. Mr. Hayward and his uncle, Charles Barrett, a 49'er, had business in San Bernardino, and started for that place. The river was not only swollen and treacherous, but in places dangerous from quicksand. This river had to be crossed and recrossed many times before reaching San Bernardino. Mr. Hayward would have to test the stream every time before making a crossing. He would doff his trousers, hang them on the back of the wagon, and wade into the stream. He said: "It seemed as if my trousers rode on the back of the wagon most of the time."

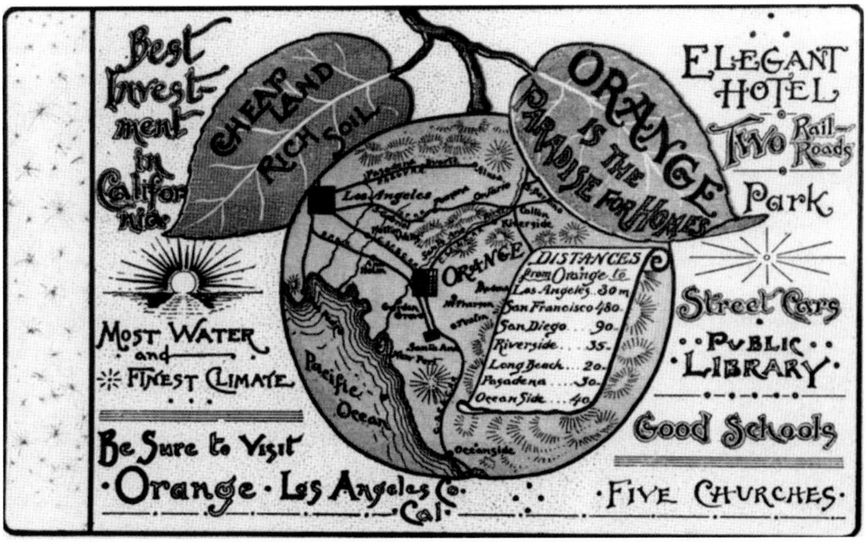

The cover of an 1888 brochure promoting the city of Orange. Selling points include easy access to water, two railroads, an "elegant hotel" and affordable and fertile farmland. Orange is described as "the best investment in California." *Courtesy the Orange Public Library.*

There are many other interesting stories about getting the mail from Anaheim when the wagon was sunk in the stream and not recovered until spring.

But the rains changed the face of old nature and brought new hope to the settler. The hills were green. Wherever a flower could burst into blossom, it did so, and thus began a new era.

People had found out there must be adequate provision for water for irrigation, and so they began the development of our splendid system.

Just before the three dry years, there had been three of plenteous rainfall, and the invitation had gone far and wide over the whole country to come to a place where an abundance of the finest products of the world could be raised and always plenty of water. There were trying times, but only a few showed any desire to give up.

Looking from our little hoes the mountains seemed so near with nothing but cactus and mustard stalks, as high as horse and rider, to measure the distance by. Mrs. Parker felt sure it would be but a pleasant walk to reach the mountains, and then have a climb. Her brother persuaded her to wait until spring when he drove her to Burruel Point (Olive). They sat at the foot of the hill in the wagon for a while. When they reached the higher ground, she saw a vast flower bed, yellow, purple, blue, and pink. There were golden poppies, and yellow composites, all kinds and sizes, the Indian paint brush, and the dainty little baby-blue-eyes.

Pioneer Life in Orange

The Loptien family, German immigrants, were very prominent in early Orange, with Mr. Loptien founding the city's first blacksmith shop. Their family's story is typical of many of the immigrant families who would have been migrating to the county during the last decades of the nineteenth century and provides invaluable insight into what the city of Orange was once like.

Mr. Henry Loptien, now eighty seven years of age, and Mrs. Loptien, seventy-eight years of age [in 1936], *were born in Germany, and, after living in Wisconsin and Illinois for six years, came to Orange in May 1884. Here they purchased ten acres of bare land from Dr. Wood, an Orange druggist. It was on the site of the first cemetery, the corner of Walnut and Cambridge. The Loptiens paid fifteen hundred dollars for the ten acres. A two-room house, kitchen, and bedroom, was on the place. There was no ceiling in the rooms except that made by the roof.*

This circa 1890 view of Orange shows numerous farmhouses dotting the landscape. Within a few decades, the landscape would quickly begin to change. This photo was taken from the tower of the Rochester Hotel. *Courtesy the Orange Public Library.*

Edwin Honey, a pioneer teamster at Orange, had brought the lumber from Newport. The view in all directions was unobstructed. The first furniture consisted of a table, two chairs, and two beds, all bought at Anaheim. The other household utensils had been brought from Illinois. The trip to and from Anaheim consumed half a day. No bridge was over the river and in the dry season the sand covered much of the wheels. Mrs. Loptien said to her husband after one of these tiresome trips: "I don't care whether I ever see Anaheim again."

The next year [1885] *Mr. Rumdahl, a Swedish carpenter who lived on La Veta, built a kitchen, a pantry, and a clothes press. He charged three dollars a day for his work.*

At first the Loptiens planted corn. When it was mature, they took the dry husks and used them to make a mattress. They had done this in Illinois. The shredded husks made a more comfortable filling than straw. The first springs they bought were purchased in Anaheim in 1887. It was a box mattress with springs. The springs and box cost twenty-eight dollars.

Loptien had been a blacksmith in Illinois. As many people said a good blacksmith was needed in Orange, Loptien built a twenty-by-thirty feet shop on the corner of his ranch. He had plenty of work to do and soon employed a man from Illinois to help him.

Then they planted a vineyard. The second year they got thirty-five dollars from it, and the third year, one hundred and fifty. The fourth year the leaves turned yellow in the summer, and the vines died. Subsequently prune trees and figs were planted. The former were bought at Anaheim and were not a success. Mr. McCoy, who lived on the ten acres across the street, had planted a good variety of figs. Each day Mrs. Loptien turned the figs and covered them, but after they were dried, they could not be sold.

The Loptiens hauled their domestic water from the ditch in a barrel. In the fall this water was not good, and Mrs. Loptien contracted typhoid fever. Soon her son became ill. They employed a German doctor from Tustin by the name of Müller. He owned twenty acres at Tustin and had come from Nebraska. One day the son swelled from the waist up, and alarmed, she called Dr. Müller. He said: "In trying to cure the typhoid, he has got the dropsy. This is what the medicine has done. It is fortunate you have called me." Another doctor employed was Dr. Medlock.

At first the Loptiens had no horse. Friends would call for them in a lumber wagon. One especially kind family was the Kamerod family, who lived at Olive.

The Loptiens were Lutherans and walked to church. It was the old two-room Lutheran church (1883) and Reverend Kogler was pastor. He had come to Orange the year before, convalescing from an operation. His salary was small, each parishioner paying what he could. But they were glad to get some one who could serve as pastor.

The church served as a school also. One Saturday night two boys knocked out all the windows in one side of the church and school. When the people came to church the next day, there were broken windows. The father of one of the boys said, "I will punish the boys myself." Whether he whipped them or shut them up, no one knew.

Four children were born to the Loptiens on this ranch. Two had been born in Illinois. This large and industrious family wanted more land. They sold the ranch for three thousand dollars, and rented land on the three hundred acres Hager Ranch on Collins and North Batavia. Mr. Hager had bought this land from John Ludermann, when Mr. Ludermann went to the Klondike. It had been a vineyard and was now used to raise barley hay.

There was a two-room house on the Hager place. The Loptiens brought their blacksmith shop and corn crib by horse and wagon to the new place. The shop is on the place now, in good repair. The crib has been destroyed. Butter was high, fifty cents a pound. The Loptiens bought it at first from Dimmicks, who lived on the present Dr. Adam's place. So the Loptiens bought four cows and some chickens and sold butter and eggs to the Ehlen and Grote wagon. The Loptiens soon tore down the old house and lived in tents, cooking in the old shop. Lumber from the old house was used in the new.

For five or six years after moving onto the new place, there was little rain, and the hay was so poor that Loptien had to make a platform on his moving machine to catch the scanty crop of hay as it fell.

This section was in great demand for orchard land and Mr. Hager was selling it off gradually. The Loptiens obtained a promise from Mr. Hager that he would not sell all of it until they had purchased a part. For the front land facing Batavia, Hager received one hundred and fifty dollars an acre. For the land in the back, one hundred and twenty five dollars. Water rights were extra.

The Loptiens finally bought twenty acres and set out walnut, apricot, and orange trees, which they purchased in Anaheim. The Travis tract of land was opposite and Mr. Brown, who had married a Mexican, and had six children, lived in a two-story house opposite. Brown was a lumberman and could give good advice as to the building of a new house.

Gradually the Loptiens sold off the twenty acres, reserving five on which they now live.

They are highly respected members of the community, as are their children and families. The old people live alone and are able to do their own work and manage their farm work.

Interview with J.E. Parker

J.E. Parker was an early pioneer to the city of Orange and one of the most helpful resources for the city's early history. Several authors compiling stories about the county during the early twentieth century remarked on his kindness and generosity with sharing his recollections of the past. Here, he reflects on his family's coming to Orange County, as well as the vibrant Mexican customs that were still a part of daily life when he was growing up.

Following the Civil War my parents, natives of Kentucky and Virginia, came to Northern California with my brothers, M.F., C.E., and C.H. and myself. My father's brother, Louis Parker, had come to Northern California in '49 and was interested in mining there. He later bought a ranch near San Jose where he had four thousand sheep. Fortune favored the family though advantageous mining ventures and good profits in sheep-raising and my father decided that he would come to Southern California and become a rancher. A pamphlet depicting the wonderful possibilities of this region played no little part in bringing about this decision. Yes, even in those long-

The Canfield Building, which served as a general merchandise store, was built in 1879. At that time, it was the first building to be built south of the Orange Plaza. *Courtesy the Orange Public Library.*

Orange's Rochester Hotel, which was replaced in the 1930s with a post office, was considered to be one of the finest hotels in Orange County. The building's striking Victorian architecture represents a style that was never widespread in the area. *Courtesy the Orange Public Library.*

gone days we had publicity in written form circulating throughout the state urging the people to settle and develop the land.

Upon arriving here in 1872, my father and the T.J. Lockhardt family, cousins of ours, purchased the old Rodriguez hacienda of 1200 acres on the Camino Real, on which property is now located the corner of North Main Street and Chapman Avenue. The Lockhardts bought from the Rodriguez heirs and then we bought the five-acre tract at Main and Chapman from them. The Parker home was built soon after we arrived, on this tract on the south-east corner of Main and Chapman. Our home was built of lumber hauled by team from San Bernardino and San Pedro. That coming from San Pedro was from the Lincoln barracks there.

There was about six-months' delay in getting possession of the Rodriguez property because of the disputes among the heirs. We lived in Anaheim in the Bremerman house until this was settled and we could build our home. The Lockhardts bought four thousand sheep from the band on the San Joaquin and continued in the sheep-raising business. We went into the nursery business.

In 1872, the time of which I speak, all of this land around what is now Orange was without trees for there was no irrigation system to make the growing of trees possible. The vast plain was used for the grazing of sheep, horses, and cattle. The only water we had for the sheep was piped through the stove-pipe to what is now the Plaza in Orange from a small dirt reservoir east of the Plaza about where Shaffer Street is at present. Each flock was allowed twenty minutes at the water, for the supply was very limited.

Life in those days was far from dull for we could always look forward to a fiesta at one of the haciendas scattered throughout the valley. These feasts took place every two or three months and sometimes oftener. In fact, every time that any member of a California family thought he had a faster horse than those of his relatives scattered throughout the state, he issued a challenge and this was taken as a signal for all to gather together for feasting, dancing, exchange of news, cock fighting, music, laughter, story telling and racing of the horses. Work was work in those days, surely, but I must say that play was most certainly play. Those happy times will never live again except in the memory of the few still living who took part in those gay events.

In the fall of the year, September 16th, Mexican Independence Day, when the most important races took place, whole families, together with their servants, would come from their homes as far north as Santa Barbara and Santa Maria and even father north than that sometimes. I remember the two Lopez boys, Benito and Juan (Chuweco, nicknamed so because he was considered tricky), were nearly always present from the Lopez ranch in Baja California. The younger men and girls rode horseback while the elderly women and very old men with the servants and many provisions, jolted along in the creaking carretas.

Twenty or thirty horses were brought along from each ranch to take part in the races and the whole herd would be turned out to graze along the river in charge of a few guards who saw to it that they stayed within bounds. This was never a difficult task for the grass was very plentiful and the animals were glad of the opportunity to eat their fill after the long journey from the home ranches.

There were a number of Basque families already here in those days, all interested in sheep-raising: Maurice Bell, who had 1200 acres east of where

Santa Fe Springs is now, the Bastanchurys of the vast rolling-hill country north of Fullerton, the Didiers, who had a part of the Workman ranch near Puente of today, Pete Nicholas from the country southwest of Fullerton, John Aleck, who had leased a portion of the old rancho that belonged to Abel Stearns one-half mile west of the County Hospital. These families all mingled with the old California families in all of their diversions.

At all of the ranches there were walled-in enclosures, some of them a hundred feet square, the same being necessary to keep livestock away from the houses and give protection to the gardens. Ramadas were built within these courtyards and the ground beneath was sprinkled with ashes and wet down with water to give a hard, smooth surface for the dances that took place every evening after the races. Sometimes it took two or three weeks of racing before the final winner was determined by the process of elimination.

There was a good race-track on the Yorba rancho up the river, another on the Serrano place between El Toro and the grade leading to the old Modjeska place in Santiago Canyon, and on the Rodriguez place where we lived. All of these courses were straight-aways one-half mile in length.

All of the horses of this period were mustangs—not very large but with the considerable speed and endurance. Horses of a better breed were later brought down from the agricultural district around Petaluma, north of San Francisco. As work animals the mustangs were useless but for racing and the other uses to which the Californians put them they were very good indeed.

As there was very little money in this district in those early days, it might be thought that the betting was rather tame. Not so; for there were the cattle, the horses, the land, and many other things of no mean value that could be wagered; such as silver-mounted saddles, spurs, fine sombreros and so on, down to the very shirt a man was wearing. Many is the time I have seen a man, his eyes glittering with excitement, skin off his shirt to wager it on the outcome of a race, while the crowd shouted, cheered, and screamed encouragement. I never heard the modern expression "I'll bet my shirt" that I don't think of those days, when it was really done.

It was the donkey races, usually held at the last, that drew the largest bets. Now, of course, these little animals absolutely refused to race under their own power, so the procedure was this: to each donkey there were six men, three on each side. The men placed their hands beneath the animal's stomach and the donkey was picked up bodily and carried forward along the course as far as the men could stagger under its own weight, severely hampered as they were by the struggles of the furious creature. Each time the animal left the ground his legs would fly out in wild kicks, his neck

The McPherson Warehouse in Orange was one of countless such structures that existed during the county's pioneer days. *Courtesy the Orange Public Library.*

A photograph of the Santa Ana and Orange Motor Railway, circa 1895. As the county developed, horse-drawn streetcars were quickly replaced by motorized transportation. *Courtesy the Santa Ana Public Library.*

twitting this way and that as he tried with all his might to bite his carriers. Long before the end of the half-mile course was reached the donkey would be screaming in rage and it took considerable agility on the part of the men to keep out of the way of his flying hoofs and snapping teeth. The onlookers would follow among each side of the track laughing hysterically, tears streaming down their faces.

Following the races for the day everyone rode to the ranch where the dance of the evening was to be. Of course they were tired and hungry and food was always ready for them. Each family had a large iron cauldron encased in adobe bricks with a chimney built underneath. This cooking arrangement was in the courtyard and sixty or seventy gallons of food could be prepared at one time. Sometimes plates were used but often the food was enfolded in a tortilla and eaten that way. Everyone, including the family of the house, ate outside. No tables were provided. Each person ate wherever he or she happened to be, either standing or sitting. They would all excitedly discuss the day's events. The food was simple, but it satisfied the pangs of hunger and have strength for the baile, or dance, that was to follow.

Soon the guitars would be playing lively music for the old Spanish dances. Ramon Yorba played the violin and played it very well, too. The women would appear, richly dressed in silks and velvets, wearing their bright rebosas and gay "Spanish" shawls imported from China.

One dance I remember that was quite distinctive, the name of which I cannot recall, was danced by a couple on a board about two feet square. They circled 'round and 'round each other and their feet never left the board. This dance was very attractive and called for considerable skill.

Following the dance, groups would leave by horseback to put up at the different ranches throughout the valley, the creak of their saddles, clink of their spurs and sound of their voices in laughter and snatches of song floating back in the balmy air of the night, growing fainter and fainter until at last all was still and another day of merrymaking was finished. A few short hours of rest followed and then the next day brought forth a renewal of activity, equally as exciting as the day before.

Chapter 5

NEWPORT BEACH

Newport Beach can trace its history back to the days before Orange County had separated itself from Los Angeles, when most cities today were either nonexistent or tiny settlements. Founded as a shipping port initially, the town developed under the markedly different visions of James Irvine and James McFadden, both of whom would play integral roles in the city's success.

The Works Progress Administration's records contain some fascinating insights into what the town was like when shipping, not tourism, formed a majority of the economy. This dynamic began to change quickly around the turn of the century, but the stories told to the WPA by local pioneers capture a unique and fleeting moment in Newport Beach's history.

McFadden's Wharf

An interview conducted with James McFadden shed much light on the founding of Newport Beach, which was home to the shipping port known as McFadden's Wharf from 1888 to 1907. The stories he recounted were then rewritten by a WPA employee.

> *About 1874, James McFadden had a load of fence lumber shipped from San Francisco by water to avoid the exorbitant railroad charges and the*

subsequent cost of cartage. As a large part of the lumber was to be used in the Gospel Swamp section, he looked about for a nearer landing than the one at Anaheim, deciding on the wharf in Newport Harbor used by D.M. Dorman and Captain Daniels as a landing place for the Vaquero.

Left: James Irvine Sr. (1867–1947), who lent his name to the city of Irvine, was one of Orange County's wealthiest landowners. At one time, he owned almost one-third of the county, including parts of Irvine, Laguna Beach, Anaheim, Tustin, Orange and Newport Beach. *Courtesy Santa Ana Public Library.*

Below: A circa 1900 photo of bathers at Newport Beach. Behind them can be seen McFadden's Landing, a lumber terminal that sparked development in the area. *Courtesy the Los Angeles Public Library.*

Before the lumber was unloaded, settlers urged him to sell them some of the lumber for their own needs. The first three steamer loads were sold before they could be landed. Thus, the McFadden Brothers found themselves engaged in the lumber business. Soon a thriving trade had been established. The wharf and warehouse which had been built on a flat piece of ground just north of the western end of the Coast Highway bridge by Dorman was purchased by McFadden in 1874.

Several difficulties were encountered because of this location and the facilities soon became inadequate to handle the business which had grown steadily for five years. Jim McFadden had a keen brain. Adjoining the lumber yard to the northeast was a triangular shaped bluff, belonging to James Irvine. Realizing the advantages to be gained by providing easy access to his warehouse, he leased this land, then petitioned the Board of Supervisors for a franchise to build and operate a loading chute, from the top of the bluff. [In his letter to the Los Angeles County Board of Supervisors, James McFadden specified that the chute would be 150 feet long and cost $1,000 to construct. McFadden also built a warehouse, as well as several smaller chutes that fed into his main chute, making the transport of cargo easier.]

A small settlement had grown up at McFadden's Landing. Robert McFadden had built a two-story dwelling a few rods to the westward;

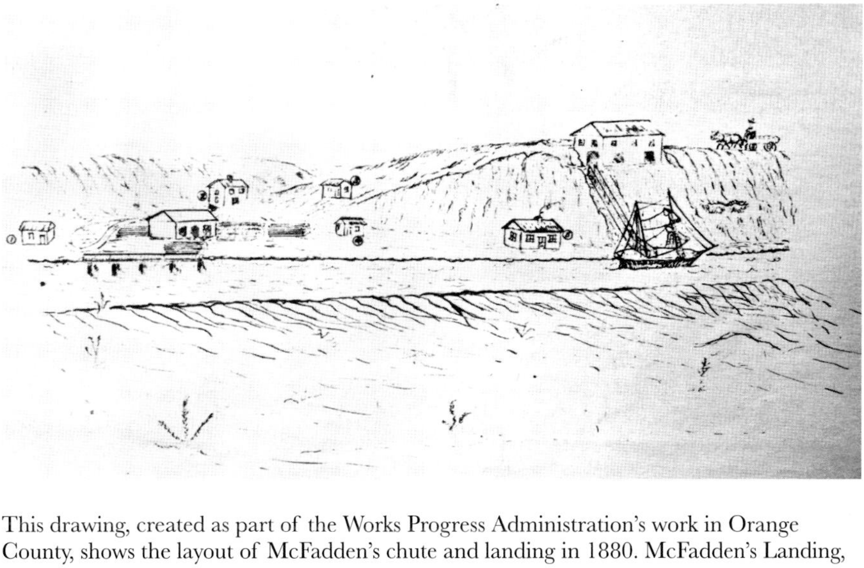

This drawing, created as part of the Works Progress Administration's work in Orange County, shows the layout of McFadden's chute and landing in 1880. McFadden's Landing, which is marked by a California State Historic plaque, evolved into present-day Newport Beach. *Courtesy the Santa Ana Public Library.*

James McMillan, who was pilot of the "Newport," started housekeeping in a cottage on the beach near the chute. A Mexican family named Saunders had a house near the bridge; Manuel, a Portuguese [immigrant], *had a cottage in back of McMillans, on rising ground; while Frank, an Italian fisherman, had a shack on the beach.*

James McFadden had the steamer "Newport" built in 1877 and for many years McFadden's Landing was a busy place. The issue of the Santa Ana Herald on June 30th, 1883 listed the cargo of the "Newport" on its current trip to San Francisco to consist of: "416 sacks of beans, 100 tons of asphalt, 23 sacks of mustard seed, 15 cases of eggs, 18 sacks of pears, 3 cases of beeswax, 3 sacks of peaches, and 80 hogs."

One great disadvantage at McFadden's Landing was the fact that storms continually changed the course of the channel by sand deposits. When Tom Rule and Mike Ortega were engaged in marking the channel preparatory to the arrival of the "Newport," their boat capsized and Rule was drowned. This tragedy, undoubtedly, had much to do with McFadden's plan to change his landing to the ocean front. In 1887 he contracted with Major Warner to build the pier which was completed the following year.

The Steamer *Newport*

McFadden's steamer, the *Newport*, played a crucial role in the early part of Orange County's history, bringing goods to and from San Francisco for many years and establishing McFadden's landing as a center of commerce. Mr. James McMillan, one of the men who worked on the steamer, was interviewed by WPA employees, who recorded his stories about the journeys up and down the coast.

James McMillan arrived in Newport in 1876. After the McFadden Brothers had the "Newport" built, he went to work on her as deckhand. After several trips he learned the coast so well, particularly the coast around Newport and the shifting channels into the harbor, that he was promoted to pilot.

Deciding to locate permanently in Newport he sent for his childhood sweetheart to come from Campbeltown [Scotland]. *They were married in Santa Ana October 30, 1880. Her maiden name was Mary McMillan, but as James, her husband, expressed it, "She's no blood*

Ships docked at Newport Beach, circa 1890. *Courtesy the Santa Ana Public Library.*

relation—an entirely different breed of cats." The newly married couple started home-keeping in a cottage built on the beach near the chute at McFadden's Landing.

John arrived in San Pedro in January 1881. He met and married Miss Annie Mills. He went to work as deckhand on the "Newport" shortly after his marriage. At that time the "Newport" stopped at every "nook and corner" between McFadden's Landing and San Francisco. The

A train can be seen on the Newport Beach pier, while in the foreground beachgoers in formal attire stand on the platform. *Courtesy the Los Angeles Public Library.*

> *usual order in the northward trip was* [from south to north]*: Anaheim Landing, San Pedro, "Portagee" Bend, Hueneme, Oxnard, Ventura (called then San Buenaventura), Santa Barbara, Santa Paula Landing, Golita, Gaviota, Lompoc (now Surf), Moro Bay, Cayucos, Port Hartford (San Luis Obispo), San Simeon, Monterey, Watsonville, Santa Cruz, Half Moon Bay, and San Francisco.*
>
> *At San Francisco, after landing their cargo of agricultural products, the steamer would take a load of lumber and assorted merchandise. This would be unloaded at the Newport wharf. Then the steamer would be moved out into the channel, directly under the long chute leading to a second warehouse built on a bluff about eighty feet high. Practically all grain, corn, and barley would be brought to the second warehouse by the teams from the surrounding ranches.*

James McMillan's Heroic Rescue

James McMillan played a role in one of the most exciting incidents in Newport's early history. One of McMillan's contemporaries recounted the story to the WPA.

James McMillan—seen here with his wife and brother, John (left), in old age—was the hero described in the sinking of one of the steamer *Newport*'s dories. The McMillan family was one of the most fondly remembered families of early Newport Beach. *Courtesy the Santa Ana Public Library.*

The story of the drowning of Captain Pierce, Mr. Cash, the ship's clerk, and two sailors at Newport, April 18, 1878 and the heroism of Mr. James McMillan, who rescued the mate and two of the crew, was recently related by Mr. A.T. Cole, the pioneer of Greenville [now part of Costa Mesa]. *Mr. McMillan made the rescue alone as the other men witnessing the disaster refused to go out in the rough sea which caused the accident.*

Mr. McMillan was somewhat reluctant to tell the story in which he took such a heroic part. However, he was persuaded to supply the following details. The steamer "Newport" was returning from the north with a heavy cargo. It had stopped at the San Pedro Harbor, where Captain Pierce was notified relative to the water conditions at Newport. The steamer timed its arrival in Newport in order to take advantage of the highest waters on that day to enter the bay. It arrived about daybreak April 18. The ocean was very rough and the "breakers" unusually high.

When the "Newport" was loaded with a heavy cargo, it was the custom to send some of the officers in to consult the pilot as to the best method to follow in landing the freight. Often lumber would be thrown in the ocean, made into rafts and then floated to land. At other times a lighter would be sent out and enough of the cargo taken off in this manner to lighten the "Newport" so that it could steam up to the warehouse. Often the steamer was lodged on the sand, advancing a little as each high swell would float it and little by little finally reach the wharf.

On the morning of the eighteenth the mate and two of the crew started for the shore in a row boat to consult the men on the lighter as to the best course to pursue in landing the steamer.

When they reach the breakers the boat capsized. It was apparent to the men on the lighter as well as those on the "Newport," that unless given immediate help three men would drown.

Mr. McMillan promptly sprang into a dory and called for volunteers to go to the rescue of the men struggling for their lives in the water. As the ocean was so rough many of the dozen men on the lighter responded.

Undaunted and alone Mr. McMillan managed to reach them and dragged the three men into the boat over the stern, the mate unconscious, and landed them safely on the beach.

His next problem was to resuscitate the rescued men. There was nothing on the level sand that could be used, so Mr. McMillan called on the men, now eager to help, for assistance. Lying down, he directed them to roll the victims over his back and in this manner the water they had swallowed was forced out and all were revived.

The crew remaining on the "Newport" had seen the accident, so Captain Pierce, Mr. Cash, the ship's clerk, and two of the crew started for the scene of the accident and a metallic life-boat. Mr. McMillan recalls that it "rode high" and seeing them coming in obliquely, instead of square with the breakers, called out to the men on shore, to go to their help as he knew they too would be capsized as soon as they reached the breakers.

Concentrating his attention to restoring the men he had brought ashore, Mr. McMillan did not see the Captain's boat capsize as he predicted. The four men in the life-boat were all drowned because of their heroic attempt to save the men of their crew, who had been rescued by Mr. James McMillan. At a banquet given to him at Long Beach by the grateful men whose lives he had saved, Mr. McMillan said he felt more at home on the water than he did at the celebration.

The shipwreck was significant enough to be covered in Los Angeles's newspapers in the days following the event. Dredging of the harbor and the construction of breakwaters during the 1930s ensured that such a tragedy would not occur again.

Other Newport Beach Tales

James McMillan also recounted other memories from his first years in Newport Beach; as with his other recollections, the stories were rewritten by the WPA before being included in its work.

In the upper bay at Newport was Sulphur Spring. Frequently a small boat would be towed up to the spring. A V-shaped trough was arranged so as to conduct the water to the boat. The water ran so slowly it would take twenty-four hours to fill the boat. The next day they would go up to the spring again and tow the boat back, the people helping themselves to the water. Many cures have been reported from using this Sulphur Spring water, but the spring is dry now [as of 1936].

Many interesting incidents occurred in which these two old timers [James McMillan and his brother, John] *took an active part. One day after the new ocean pier had been built, five whales, pursued by a school of black-fish* [orcas] *came very close in shore. When the whales realized they were being driven onto the beach, they turned around and churning the*

This 1890 photograph shows the McFadden brothers, along with a contractor, constructing a bridge over the Santa Ana River for the Santa Ana & Newport Beach Railroad. The railroad allowed McFadden's Wharf to develop at a very brisk pace. *Courtesy the Los Angeles Public Library.*

McFadden's pier in Newport Beach in about 1895. One of the men (fourth from right) on the right side of the picture is Mr. James McMillan. *Courtesy the Santa Ana Public Library.*

water to foam and spouting, formed in a line five abreast and raced out to sea. Frequently whales came up and spouted close to the "Newport." Once a whale, coming up beside the steamer, rubbed against the boat attempting to scrape off some of the barnacles which dotted his side. One of the passengers wanted to shoot the whale but the captain forbid it because it was so close that the captain feared the steamer might be damaged by the huge tail of the whale, even in his death struggle.

Another time when out in his skiff a whale came to the surface so near James McMillan's boat that when he spouted the water drenched his clothes.

Seals were very numerous at the mouth of the inlet to Newport Bay. At times James McMillan estimates that he had seen over a thousand seals sunning themselves on the sand at the inlet. If a human being approached within gun shot, a wild scrambling occurred as the seals flapped their way into the water. Occasionally a fur-bearing seal—a straggler from northern waters—would be seen among them.

On one occasion Mrs. James McMillan found a baby seal on the beach. It is presumed that on the rare occasions when a seal gives birth to twins they abandon the weaker. She picked up the seal and carried it home, keeping it in a cage her husband built for it. She fed it milk and succeeded in keeping it alive for some time but it died after a few days.

Living at McFadden's Landing was a fisherman named Manuel Dabney who had a reputation as a teller of tall tales. Many were the adventurous yarns he spun.

Dabney claimed that years ago Newport Bay was a favorite hiding place for pirates. For many years there was a cave on the eastern side of the inlet (where Corona del Mar is now) which was used by the pirates and in which they kept a sharp lookout for potential prizes or possible pursuer. It was claimed by Dabney that a passage led from the cave to the heights above. The inlet, turning sharply as it does, offered complete coverage for the pirates' ships.

It was the fishermen's custom after killing a shark, removing the liver and cutting off the fins, to leave it on the beach or in the water close by where the tide would wash it ashore. These decaying carcasses were so numerous that the stench arising from them polluted the air for miles. On one occasion the Moesser family was visiting the beach, having as guests several deaf and dumb girls. As they sailed along the shore the girls soon proved that their sense of smell was super-normal. They became quite excited and talked rapidly with their fingers.

On one occasion John McMillan saw a shark swimming near the Newport pier that was between twenty-five and thirty feet long. At the side of his nose swam a diminutive pilot fish. It is believed that these pilot fish touch the nose of the shark to steer him toward food or warn him of approaching danger. Owing to his very small, pig-like eyes, the shark is unable to see in any direction but straight ahead. When following a boat of any kind, sharks invariably swim on the lee quarter. It is considered great sport by sailors to catch a shark just to see "what it has in his pocket." A piece of meat is securely attached to a large hook and thrown overboard. Mr. Shark greedily gulps it down. He is then drawn up to the side of the boat and dispatched with spears. Then his stomach is cut open. Sharks have a habit of swallowing anything shiny. As a result sailors would occasionally find coins, rings, and jewelry in the shark's "pocket."

Quite a few sharks were found in the water south of Newport and the fishermen were always on the look-out for their triangular dorsal fins cutting the water. The shark's liver yielded a generous quantity of oil and their fins brought a good price when shipped to China where they were regarded as a choice tid-bit and delicacy. "Portagee" Bend—so called because of the number of Portuguese fishermen living there, was the headquarters of the shark hunters.

Another man they found living at the Landing was Joe Serro, a native of Chile, who claimed to have a gold mine in Lucas Canyon. Serro said the padres had found considerable gold in Capistrano Creek, which undoubtedly had washed down from the canyons above. He claimed that gold had been sometimes brought to the mission by Indians and that the gold supply thus accumulated was sent to Rome.

Mr. Brockett's Memories of Newport Beach

Mr. C.W. Brockett was another Orange County pioneer and first moved west from La Harpe, Illinois, to Santa Ana in 1885. The following year, his family relocated once again, this time several miles away to the newly formed community of Newport Beach. His childhood years left him with many memories about what life was like shortly after the McFadden brothers began their new settlement.

My family moved to Newport in 1886, when the place was nothing but sand piles nearly as high as a house. My father was the first post-master, and built the first bath-house and store.

The bay was full of clams, scallops, mussels, and the fishermen sold to anyone who wished to buy. Croakers, smelt, and suckers were caught with a seine. Yellowtail, barracuda, and mackerel were also abundant. There was no law then against fishing as there is now.

The seine was fifteen-hundred feet long, twenty-four feet high in the center, and five feet at each end. The boat carried seven-hundred feet of rope, which was fastened to the end of the seine. The men would row beyond the breakers, before the seine would lie out flat. Then they would go up and down the beach catching fish. When the seine was full, a horse hitched to the rope would pull the fish in. It took four men, and a team to pull in the catch.

Sometimes there were so many fish in the nets that men had to wade into the water to lay the lead line on the bottom and the cork line on top in order to raise the seine, and let out some of the fish. As the fish poured out, the force of their movement almost tore the men's legs off.

The fish brought one to four cents per pound. They were boxed and sent to Los Angeles.

This was the time when sailing ships brought in lumber. The Santa Fe [Railroad] *obtained its bridge timber and railroad ties here. There*

An early view of Newport Beach visitors, taken in the summer of 1891. Pyramidal tents that once lined the beachfront can be seen behind them. *Courtesy California State University, Fullerton.*

This photograph, taken by the Works Progress Administration, shows the site of McFadden's landing in the 1930s. Since the WPA photographed the site, it has changed immensely. *Courtesy the Santa Ana Public Library.*

> *were usually one to seven boats ready to be unloaded of Oregon and Washington pine.*
>
> *McFadden's boat, the "Newport," was a little tub about seventy-five feet long. The "Eureka" and the "Los Angeles" were wooden boats, whose trip ended at Newport. Then they returned north again.*
>
> *When business increased, and there were more passengers, and the south began to grow, the "Corona" and the "Pomona," steel ships, made the trip from San Francisco to San Diego, stopping at Newport both coming and going. They belonged to the Pacific Steamship Company. Four ships capable of carrying passengers came regularly each week to Newport.*
>
> *In 1887 there were several wild cat schemes to promote industries at Newport, one of which was a glass factory on the top of the sand hill on the west side of town. But the sand was not the right kind for glassmaking.*

Eventually, McFadden sold his wharf and railroad to the Southern Pacific Railroad, and by 1902, he had sold all the land he owned in the area. It was during this time that Newport Beach was quickly transformed from a commercial shipping center into a resort destination. The coming of the Red Car in 1905 and the construction of the Balboa Pavilion in 1906 furthered this shift. By the time Newport Beach was founded in August 1906, McFadden's Wharf and chute remained only as a memory in the minds of the city's pioneers.

Chapter 6

THE CANYONS

The numerous canyons in the Santa Ana Mountains still form the most remote region of Orange County. Sparsely populated dating back into the middle of the nineteenth century, these canyons were home to countless hunting expeditions, mining claims and various other hopeful opportunists trying to strike it rich. While most of these attempts never materialized into anything lucrative, the stories shared by the pioneers of the canyons represent an invaluable chapter of the county's history.

A Grizzly Bear Hunt in Orange County

The thought of grizzly bears in Orange County may seem far-fetched today—the last grizzly seen in California was in 1924, and that was in the Sierras. But for much of the nineteenth century, these animals were incredibly common, with one study estimating that there were once ten thousand grizzlies throughout the state. Orange County's mountainous regions provided a perfect habitat, and more than a few early settlers recall seeing them. Not all pioneers, though, had the same experience that Mr. N.T. Wood had in Santiago Canyon in 1869. His harrowing tale reads like a pulp fiction story.

> *All of my life I have liked to hear the report of burnt powder. Even early as eight or nine years old when there was nothing but the old flint lock gun.*

First Street between Santa Ana and Tustin. In the distance is a horse-drawn carriage, while along the side of the road is an irrigation ditch, instrumental for agriculture in early Orange County. *Courtesy California State University, Fullerton.*

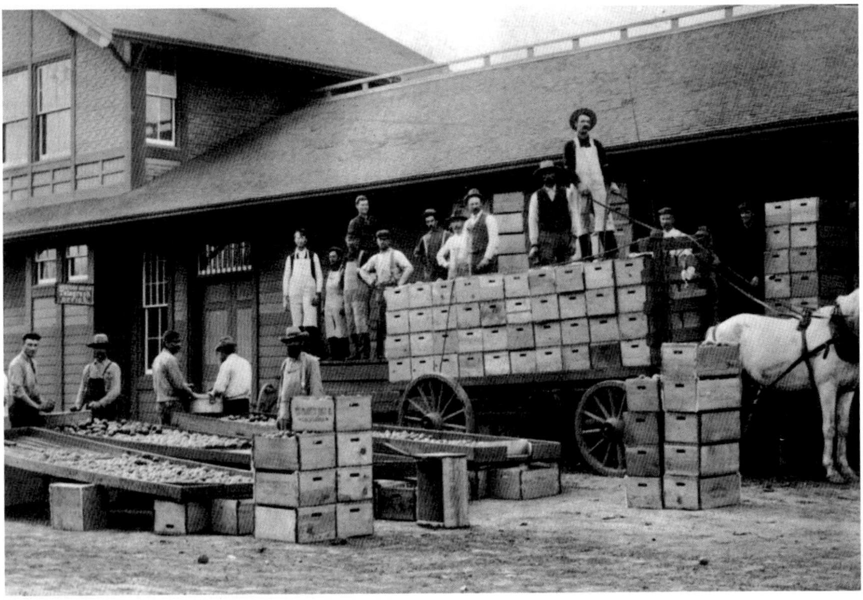

Men are seen packing crops in this circa 1915 photograph from Tustin. The structure seen behind them was the city's early depot. *Courtesy the Orange County Public Library.*

When we had no flit, I would load 'er up, and with my cousin (about my own age) would go hunting. I would hold her on the game (chipmunk) and he would touch 'er off with a coal of fire. In 1865 I bought a six shooter, a Henry rifle from the first lot shipped to California paying sixty-five dollars. It was poorly sighted so I resighted it and screwed it in a vice and sighted it for a two hundred yard target and made six shots before moving it from the vice, and a silver dollar would have covered the six shots.

In 1869 I was living in the Santiago Canyon about twenty miles distant from the coast. For two years there had been forest fires in the high range mountains that had driven the game towards the coast. At this date the country was covered with Mexican land grants from Anaheim to San Luis Rey, a distance of over fifty miles without a settlement whatsoever, except the grant houses which were a long distance apart. My trading post was at Anaheim, thirty miles distant. One day when I was in for supplies I met a man driving two horses hitched to a spring wagon and leading a monster stallion nearly eighteen hands high. In talking to him, I found he was from Oregon. He had come to California to exhibit his horse. I says to him, "I am living alone in the mountains thirty miles from here, won't you go home with me and rest up for a few days?"

He slapped his hands together and says, "That's just what suits me." I said, "I can give you all the venison you want to eat." "I would like to get a chance at a deer myself," says he. We both bought supplies and the next day he went home with me. I had a garden and was experimenting on tobacco raising. My visitor's name was Davis. Mr. Davis told me something about Oregon. He said it rained or snowed there the year round and told me you could tell an Oregonian whenever you met him, for he would take off his hat and shake water from it.

We got here about four o'clock. I have a big lonely camp with big live oak and sycamore trees especially, with a small stream of running water about a hundred yards from the cabin. [Mr. Wood was one of the first settlers in Santiago Canyon. Nicknamed "Tule Woods," he was a noted hunter, miner and mountaineer. Later in life, he lived in Trabuco Canyon before passing away in National City at the age of ninety-eight.]

After staying here one day, Mr. Davis was anxious to get a deer so we packed things for camping and drove up the canyon and camped for a hunt. All next day we hunted faithfully and never saw a deer, they had been run off the range by some means. I says to Mr. Davis, "About three miles from here are where the bears range, and they are numerous here now, how would you like a bear hunt?" "That suits me exactly," says he. "I have killed a good many bear in Oregon."

Grizzly bears were once common in Southern California, as evidenced by the story recounted in this volume. This etching shows a typical hunt during the nineteenth century; lassos were often used to capture the animal alive. *Courtesy the Los Angeles Public Library.*

Now Mr. Davis was poorly armed for a bear hunt. He had a double barreled gun, one for shot, and the other barrel was a rifle. Also a sawed off shot gun which he carried in a scabbard buckled around him.

Now I would like to describe the disposition of the grizzly bear for who ever may read this. When all four feet are on the ground, they can see but a few feet ahead of them, but when they are disturbed they stand on their hind legs to see at a distance, and they will never tackle a person before standing up. If you come on to a grizzly in the open country and say if he is a hundred yards away, if you stand still he is apt to go away, but if you start for him he will surely come to meet you.

There is one thing more the hunter will never forget.

If you wound a grizzly you will never lose him, for he will hunt for you as long as he has life to crawl.

We started on our bear hunt early in the morning and when we were near to where I expected to find them I told Mr. Davis to go up to the main canyon from the north, and to go up the stream, and I would go over the ridge and wait for him above. So where I went, there was a patch of open country without tree or brush, on a gentle sloping hill that sloped toward the creek. I was standing two hundred yards from the creek when I saw two bears coming down the creek toward me. They were out of sight most of the time until they were opposite of me, when one of them came out on the bank and stood broadside with his head down stream. They had never dreamed that I was waiting for them with sixteen loads in the gun and a pocket full of cartridges. I had a good chance and I aimed for the heart and I found out later the bullet went about two inches back of it.

The bear fell into a pool of water and bawled, but it came right out, stood up and saw me, and on it came with bloody mouth as if nothing had happened.

For the third time I shot him as the other bear came from the creek and smelt the blood and bawled fearfully and followed number one down until he fell over and never got up again. She pawed the dead bear as if to wake him up, then stood up and saw me and on she came. I shot her while running and sent her to the creek, but she was after me in an instant and when she first started I shot her again, but still she rallied and came for the third shot, and when she was about a hundred yards below me—pop—pop.

That was my first thought of Mr. Davis being on the job. He never touched the bear, but came near to hitting me. Now this bear started for Mr. Davis on a straight line between him and me and had about seventy five yards to go and Davis stood there like a post.

In an instant I knew what I must do, I must kill that bear or Davis would be chewed up. It would be dangerous to shoot her while she was running, so I was ready when she stood up and I made the shot that saved Davis. The bear fell, I had broke her neck and I hurried over to see the situation. The bear lay about eight feet from Davis breathing her last, still struggling to get to him. Mr. Davis had never moved. I says to him, "Why in ---- are you standing here for? Did you expect me to take chances in hitting you or the bear? Why didn't you get on that ledge of rocks or climb that tree?" Now Mr. Davis didn't speak—didn't move—he was paralyzed—chained to the spot. I shook him and pulled him away from there and went to skinning the bear.

Pretty soon he took out his knife and helped skin the two bears. We hung up on a tree the two hides and some of the meat and started for camp.

"That is a wonderful gun of yours," says he, "and a wonderful man to shoot it. I saw some of your shooting before I shot but I was sure the bear would get to you. They are not like our Oregon bears. I have never seen any like them." We went and moved camp to with-in half a mile of where the bears were hung and camped for the night.

In the morning Mr. Davis hitched up and started up the creek for the bear hides. Now there is a piece of flat country and the creek has a perpendicular bank that about hides the teams and I went on the flat, above. There is neither tree nor brush in this flat and not more than two hundred yards away was a monster bear in a clover patch; when he heard the wagon he stood up and saw me and made a few jumps toward me, but I stood still and he started away, but every few jumps he raised up to see if I was coming, I think he would have weighed nine hundred to a thousand pounds and if I had shot him there would have been a large amount of trouble.

The two we killed were yearlings, weight about four hundred pounds a piece.

In going along to keep up with the wagon I saw another monster, but he was some distance away. We got the hides and some of the meat and got home all right.

When Mr. Davis was leaving I says to him, "Whenever you want another bear hunt call around."

Smiling, he thanked me for my kindness and took of his hat to shake the water from it.

Although Santiago Canyon has been free of grizzly bears for more than a century, there is still one place you can find them in Orange County—albeit in name only. Local legend has it that Oso Parkway in Mission Viejo was named after the county's former denizens. Locals can still see bears at the Orange County Zoo, although they are of the black bear variety—not originally native to the region and much smaller than the monsters that Mr. Wood used to hunt.

Nature Stories of Santiago Canyon

Although still celebrated for hiking trails and untouched wilderness, the Santa Ana Mountains and other parts of inland Orange County were once home to a much wider variety of wild animals than today. Here, one pioneer recounts just what kinds of wildlife were commonplace more than one hundred years ago.

Andrew Joplin, born in Virginia in 1864, and located on Judge Montgomery's place east of El Modena, was interviewed and told the following story concerning wild game in Santiago Canyon:

Grizzly bears were plentiful in Santiago Canyon as they were fond of the acorns which were plentiful especially around what is now Irvine Park. They even climbed some of the oak trees to get the acorns. Mr. J.E. Pleasants killed one there that weighed eight hundred pounds. There were also lots of big wolves. The bee men killed a great number of bears and wolves by setting out poison.

A large number of antelope used to range around where Fullerton and Anaheim are now located.

Mr. Joplin saw his last condor about 1923. In his boyhood days they had been quite common. He would see several every day. They measured about nine feet six inches from wing tip to wing tip.

They roosted at the head of Trabuco Canyon, where the Indians would go to find the feathers which they had shed. The Indians prized these large feathers highly. Later the bee men used to go there to get the feathers to use for brushing their bees off the honey.

Occasionally a golden eagle would be seen sitting on some dead animal surrounded by a ring of condors, which were also surrounded, further back, by a circle of turkey buzzards, all waiting their turn to get something to eat.

Mr. Joplin says there are still some condors in Lower California and some have been reported to have been seen recently in Santa Barbara and Ventura Counties.

Buzzards live on dead animals which they find, but Mr. Joplin has seen them kill skunks. Several would surround the skunk and would pick out first one eye, then the other; when totally blind, it was easy to finish. He also once saw a lamb that had been killed by buzzards in the same manner.

He observed woodpeckers about Irvine Park put accords in the bark of trees, they would drill a hole in the bark, then fly down to the ground, and after some time fly up with an accord that would exactly fit the hole drilled. The accord selected would fit with an exactness, as if measured with a delicate instrument.

Sherman Stevens of Tustin once shot a Blue Goose, the only one known to have been killed in Orange County.

Mr. Joplin was told a story by a man, who claimed to have seen it in the mining country up north, of a battle royal. The miners had secured an African Lion, and put it in a pen with a grizzly bear which promptly killed the lion, they then turned a bull loose in the pen. The bull paid no attention to the bear, but ran around looking for a way out. The bear got in front of it and stood up, whereupon the bull charged the bear and gored it through the chest with its long horn killing it instantly. The bull seemed unconcerned and went on looking for a place to get out.

J.E. Parker's Story of Mining in Silverado

In 1876, the Santa Ana Mountains experienced a silver rush when word spread that nuggets of ore had been found. J.E. Parker, one of the first men responsible for the mineralogical discovery, recounted his entire story to WPA workers.

In 1874 my brother and I were hunting deer in the head of the canyon now known as Harding and were resting at the pot holes, which were formed by the water falling over ledges, that crossed the canyon. This was about three miles up the canyon from Shrewsberry's bee ranch, where we were camping.

At one of these holes we noticed some small round metal nuggets, which were bright and heavy. We picked up quite a few of them and brought them back to our camp. They were about the size of walnuts and smaller.

Sam Shrewsberry had seen lead in Missouri and said it was lead. We put some in an oak wood fire and melted it.

Then we returned to the holes and looked the place over. It was almost at the top of the ridge. On the north side was the canyon known as "the Silverado." Picking up more of the nuggets, we brought them to Orange.

We had been buying shot and bullets from the Selby Smelting Company of San Francisco, and decided to send some of the nuggets. We picked out the darkest of them, filled a ten pound shot sack, and sent it to them.

In three weeks we received a letter from them, saying it was galena ore and carried fifty-two dollars in silver. They said they were greatly interested in the ore and would send two men down to look it over. They offered to pay us well for any assistance we could give them. They would come by boat to San Pedro.

We met them there, loaded their baggage, and implements, and started for Sam Shrewsberry's cabin, where we set up camp.

As the inspectors wished to camp on the ground under examination, we packed the horses and went to the pot holes.

We remained there three weeks, thoroughly covering all the mineral ground.

These two men were thirty-five years old; one, a graduate of the Colorado School of Mines, the other, a graduate of Pittsburg Mining School. They had been with Selbys for five years, and had been everywhere in search of lead and silver.

In the morning we would start out in different directions for the day, bring a sample of any rock or ledge that looked favorable. We covered all the country from Saddleback down to Lodi Canyon.

These two inspectors were goats to climb but they had nothing on us boys. They were thorough and being with them for three weeks was an education.

Having located six well-defined claims, we broke camp, and returned home.

The Selby Smelting Company sent us five hundred pounds of shot, one hundred pounds of powder, one thousand rounds of ammunition for Winchester rifles. The two men sent us a fine loading machine for loading shells.

When the men returned to San Francisco, they took one hundred pounds of dried venison.

They sent me a printed report of their findings. It stated that the mineral belt was one mile wide by two miles long, and the mineral was of a sulphate character, of no great deposit, and would require smelting.

We came down home, did up our work and went back to the mines. We ran and established our lines, put up the corners, put up our notices and named the Santiago district. We elected a recorder, laid out Santiago City, now covered by Modjeska Lake. We returned to the mines and selected nuggets from the pot holes. We did not take the bright metallic ones. The men had shown us what to select, the brown and dark ones that carried the most value. We took the horses up and packed down about one ton of the metal, which we brought down home and shipped from San Pedro to Selbys in San Francisco.

One day in Anaheim, I met Mr. Pellegrin, a jeweler, who wanted to know where I had been and what I was doing. I told him about the mines and that we had staked eight claims under the advice of Selbys. He became very much interested and wanted some of the ore. I happened to have a nugget in my pocket, and I showed it to him.

"Come," he said, "let's try the torch on it."

The torch melted the lead and left a filagree of silver standing. We put the latter into a cupel and melted it to a button, which Pellegrin weight on a jeweler's scale and found it worth three hundred dollars per ton. And that was what Selby and Company returned for the ton shipped to them.

Pellegrin became very much excited and wanted to go to the hills at once, but we delayed going there for three days. He came past our home with a team and wagon loaded with a camp outfit good for a month's stay in the hills.

NOTICE!

We did not go to Shrewsberry's but turned up the wooded canyon now known as Silverado Canyon. We packed up the canyon opposite to the pot holes to get the lay of the country as well as samples. We traced the edge back north-west over the top of the ridge and found the out-crop of ledge. We located several mining claims, posted notices, and ran lines on the border of these claims.

Some of these samples assayed very well, and it soon became noised around that we had found silver.

Then the rush started. Of all the different kinds of outfits from one horse wagons, two horse wagons, buggies, carts, mule packs, to men walking with donkeys, packing all their worldly goods, and then some just walking, all going—no one knew where. Most of them did not know a nugget from a potato. Farmers from the [Gospel] *Swamp, vineyardists from Anaheim, cattlemen, San Bernardino carpenters, painters, plasterers, bricklayers, plumbers, mostly with their families, but no miners.*

Summer was coming, and the weather was fine. Everybody was rich suddenly, and very happy. They were building cooking ovens, and setting up tents. The men dug a ditch from the crick to a flat, and the women and children were irrigating and planting gardens. The men brought in the deer. They were truly happy. One woman said she didn't care if her husband didn't get one ounce of silver. This trip was worth more to her and her children than all the silver in the hills.

One man said that everyone was so happy and was singing, and that the general atmosphere reminded him of a Methodist camp meeting. That was quite a record for a mining camp.

They were coming in more rapidly now, and the men decided to establish a law and helping club. They decided to have no saloons in Santiago or Silverado cities. People must do all cooking in cooking ovens, and have no fires, and when in the hills, must carry a canteen of water, and be very careful of fire.

To help them, we decided to place a man at the forks of the canyons to instruct them where to go to camp, give them mining blanks, show them how to fill them out, and give them any knowledge we possessed.

Opposite, top: A nineteenth-century photograph of one of Silverado Canyon's numerous mines. For a brief time, Silverado Canyon was something of a boomtown; however, many hopeful prospectors were unable to strike it rich. *Courtesy the Anaheim Public Library.*

Opposite, bottom: Carbondale, located near Silverado Canyon, was one of numerous prospective boomtowns during the second half of the nineteenth century. Although the community had a post office for a short while, all that remains today is a California State Historic marker. *Courtesy the Orange County Archives.*

I went up to the pot holes and got a lot of nuggets—and gave one to the prospector, so that he would know what to look for. I told them it was a sulphate camp, and nothing else had been found of any moment or value.

They were grateful. I met many fine fellows and their ladies. One day I came down to the forks, and there I met a man and his wife with their two children. The man was off to one side, sitting on a rock and smoking a corncob pipe. His wife was at the cooking fire.

Walking up to the man, who weighted two hundred and twenty-five pounds, was very florid and had sandy hair, I said, "Good morning, are you going mining?"

He replied: "I reckon I like to mine."

"Where are you from?" I said.

"From Texas, and when pap came to Cal, I followed the wagon to see if the big wheel'd ketch the little one."

"Where do you live now?"

"In the hills back of San Bernardino, raising some cattle."

The wife left her cooking and came over to where we were, and said: "What's that feller talking to you about?"

"He says them hills up there has a lots of silver in 'em."

"Well, it can stay in 'em, they're too high for me."

"Well, Jen, you stay in camp, and I'll go up there and dig up a whole lot of silver and we'll be rich."

A Mr. Prothoro, along with other unidentified men and women, is seen in front of a large piece of farm equipment on the Irvine Ranch. *Courtesy the Los Angeles Public Library.*

An aerial view of part of Irvine Ranch, which was founded by Mr. James Irvine in 1864. *Courtesy the Los Angeles Public Library.*

A band of cowboys is seen watching a herd of cattle in southern Orange County. Sights such as this were once common throughout the region. *Courtesy the Orange County Archives.*

"Pa told me before we was married you wouldn't dig potatoes. You was lazy, trifling, but I told pa, if I could get you, I'd make you work. Now you would go up on one of them hills where I couldn't holler to you. When you come down at night, I would ask what you were settin' for. You said waiting for the rain, and when it rained you went back a settin' to see the grass grow."

Jim sat on his rock grinning a happy grin. He seemed to think it a part of married life.

I told them to drive up the canyon for six miles and camp. "And when you go prospecting be sure your fires are out, and, Jim, when you go up a side canyon, build a mound of rock and put a note on it, stating the time you left, so if anything happens to you, we will know where to look for you. The canyons are steep and you might fall and break a leg."

"What! Jim get his leg broke! And the snakes will bite the children! You are not going one step. We are going back to the pa and ma, and you are going to work."

"Don't Jen me, it don't do no good."

Jim kept on grinning. I wished I was big, red headed, and good natured. Life seemed so pleasant to Jim. He turned to me and said with a plaintive tone: "This ain't the first fortune I been beat out of."

"Beat out of nothing," said Jen, "You hain't never had anything to be beat out of. You have been trying for four years to make up your mind what to do. I ain't going to make it up for you, and you aren't going to work."

I left them debating, but as they never registered any claim, I suppose Jen got the best of the argument, and I hope she kept Jim down on level ground where she could talk to him.

One day going over the hills I came to a little level flat, and there were two men digging a hole in the middle of the flat. They were from Compton and said they were going to dig down to the bowels of the earth and see what was in 'em. It was no use to dig up in them rocks when there was good dirt to dig in.

The county was well-prospected from Santa Ana to Trabuco Creek. A few prospects looked good, but most of them were not of much moment.

We did not have any fires or troubles of any kind or hardships. We enjoyed life immensely. It remained for the tourist of a later day to go to banquets, fill up on cheap food, and cheaper speeches, and go to the hills and start fires.

About this time the mining camp, Calico, was discovered about twelve miles back of Camp Cady on the desert [San Bernardino County], *and all the miners went out there and the hills seemed lonesome.*

Chapter 7

SAN JUAN CAPISTRANO AND LAGUNA BEACH

The city of San Juan Capistrano is home to Orange County's only Franciscan mission, which was founded on November 1, 1776. Father Serra's Chapel, located on the property, was erected in 1782 and is the oldest building in the entire state that is still in use. The chapel is also the only building still standing where it is known that Father Serra celebrated Mass.

With the ruins of the mission as its nucleus, the town of San Juan Capistrano retained its Mexican heritage much longer than other parts of Orange County. As the stories compiled by the WPA show, customs such as bullfighting and horse racing persisted until the very end of the nineteenth century. A section titled "Boom Period," which describes the county as a whole, is also included in this chapter due to its description of several boomtowns that were formerly located in the proximity of San Juan Capistrano and Laguna Beach.

Marco Forster

One of the prominent men interviewed by the Works Progress Administration in the southern part of the county was Marco Forster, whose lineage in Southern California's early history is most remarkable. His grandfather Don Juan Forster moved to California in 1833 and became one of the largest landowners in the region. Marco recounted

An early photograph of Mission San Juan Capistrano, which was the seventh of California's twenty-one missions to be founded. *Courtesy the Orange County Archives.*

to the WPA some of his early recollections of living in the community of San Juan Capistrano.

> *Marco Forster is the grandson of Don Juan Forster, who once owned the Trabuco by grand form Pio Pico (Governor) in 1846, as a rancho of five leagues. This rancho had been given to Santiago Arguello, who had been administrator of the San Juan Capistrano Mission. It was given to Arguello in 1841 but the grant was never completed and he sold his rights to Don Juan Forster in 1843.*
>
> *Regarding the adobe, he recollects that Juan Erroqui lived there and others perhaps. He believes that Juan Erroqui found treasures in the old adobe.*
>
> *There was a young boy who worked for Erroqui at that time, whose people lived at San Juan Capistrano. The father of this boy was known to Marco Forster and he told Marco how the boy had been showing some gold and silver coins which he said had been given to him by Erroqui. The boy's father punished him severely and told him to take them back, believing that he had stolen them. A very short time later, Erroqui and his partners sold out and went back to the old country, the Pyrenees. Bernardo Erreca and Miguel lived there after that.*

Marco Forster believes the adobe was built by the Mission Indians and is one of those who cling to the belief that there was a Mission Vieja adobe, used by the Mission Fathers as a sort of stopping place while ministering the Indians. He claims there is proof of this.

During the "Boom" the Santa Fe [Railroad] *came through to "San Juan-by-the-Sea." This was a "Boom" subdivision. There was a pavilion built at the point. This was later partly washed away by the sea and the rest was torn down. There were excursions from San Bernardino and Riverside and Redlands. There was a "Boom" hotel also but the definite location and the builder are not known. The Santa Fe still owns three acres here. The whole flat was sold in lots. These sold for $300 to $1,000 for each 100 feet. A large reservoir was built at that time by the city. It was ten years after the "Boom" before things were normal again.*

At San Juan Capistrano, in "Boom" time, just opposite the old stone church on the Camino Real was a building that had been brought from San Onofre. It was used as an amusement place and for dancing. It was operated by "Soto Bill" (Pablo Soto).

"San Juan-by-the-Sea" is now called Doheny Park.

During the youth of Marco Forster, he was considered the champion romper in these parts. The youths all danced well, but never taught by dancing instructors. They "just danced." Everyone rode, and they had fine saddle horses. They enjoyed a horse-race too, but the Eastern horses could always beat them. The thoroughbreds were better for distance and endurance, while these California bred horses were too easily "done." Lack of good breeding mares was the reason for this. Music was a natural accomplishment also. Almost everyone could play the guitar.

For amusements they had horse racing, cock fighting, roping contests. Every Sunday there were races, etc., held at San Juan Capistrano, and people came from long distances to take part or watch. The race track was the street, and the cock fights too, were held out in the open.

The ladies came to watch and many of them bet excitedly on their favorites. They had silks and fine cloth from Los Angeles or San Francisco brought overland.

The present home [1935] *of Marco Forster at San Juan Capistrano was moved there in 1873 from San Onofre. In his home he has a fine serape which he claims was worn by Pio Pico when he fled before the Americans into Mexico.*

Although Marco Forster's home is no longer standing in San Juan Capistrano, there now exists a middle school in that city named in his honor.

Boom Period

Many Orange County towns have come and gone over the decades. Whether unprosperous mines or poor farmland, not every community had what it takes to become a long-lasting city. Colonel Solomon Henderson Finley, who was raised in California before attending college in Illinois, was one of the civil engineers responsible for the planning and development of many of these "boomtowns." The "boom" to which Colonel Finley makes frequent reference was a real estate boom that Southern California experienced in 1887. However, the bubble burst nearly as soon as it had begun, leaving many hopeful communities abandoned and forgotten. Here, in his own words, are Finley's recollections of a few of these towns.

> *Prominent among the towns developed during the Boom was Fairview, a two hundred acre tract about three miles south of Greenville. A narrow gauge steam railroad was built to the town. The tracks ran along Fairview Avenue from the Santa Ana terminal on Broadway. This road operated for a year or two until after the collapse of the boom, at which time the tracks were taken up.*

Ladies playing tennis in Laguna Beach during the early 1880s. *Courtesy the Santa Ana Public Library.*

A crowd gathers in front of the old Laguna Beach Hotel to take a photo during the 1880s. *Courtesy the Santa Ana Public Library.*

Fairview was originally located near the intersection of Harbor Boulevard and Adams Avenue, in what is now Costa Mesa. Greenville, another community that is no longer around, still lends its name to Greenville Street in Santa Ana—about three miles north of Costa Mesa, just as Colonel Finley described.

> *Arch Beach was strictly another "Boom" town, in which the Goff Brothers were active participants. A mile below Arch Beach and west of Aliso Canyon, on the mesa, another "Boom" town called Santa Catalina-on-the-Main, sprang into being. One hundred acres or more were laid out in lots and graded. Aside from a few scattering dwellings, nothing remains.*

Arch Beach was located south of Laguna Beach, near modern-day Moss Street. The town had a post office, a general store and a hotel constructed by the Goff brothers (whom Finley references). Santa Catalina-on-the-Main, based on Finley's measurement, would have been located near Catalina Drive in Laguna Beach—whether the street name is a remnant of this long-forgotten town or merely a coincidence is unknown.

One of Orange County's lost communities, Arch Beach was located in present-day Laguna Beach. Seen here was the settlement's most prominent establishment, Goff's Arch Beach Hotel, which opened in 1886. *Courtesy the Santa Ana Public Library.*

Abalone. *Courtesy the Orange County Archives.*

> *Modena, now called El Modena, was one of the boom towns which survived, goring into a thriving community. Another development called South Santa Ana comprised 150 to 200 acres of land owned by James McFadden and others and extended from McFadden Street to Delhi Road and from McClay to Halladay Streets. Several excursions were run to the tract on the Southern Pacific Railroad from Los Angeles. Brass bands and free refreshments were usually features of these excursions. St. James, called "Jim Town," was another short-lived development center. San Juan by the Sea was laid out in 1887, at the time the Santa Fe Railroad was put through to San Diego.*

Much of El Modena has since been annexed by the city of Orange; likewise, South Santa Ana (as the name implies) is now part of Santa Ana. San Juan by the Sea, located near the mission, had a lot of potential when it was founded. The area was subdivided, homes were built and the Santa Fe Railroad even provided a spur to the beach. However, like all the towns mentioned thus far, as soon as the market burst the town dried up; its sole legacy are several street names in Dana Point that have been kept.

> *The 160 acre tract of land including the southwest corner of First and Main and extending to Flower and Fairview Streets was cut into town lots, graded, and cement sidewalks laid. When the boom broke, the sidewalks were torn up and the land turned back to acreage upon which a large crop of barley was raised. It was over fifteen years before real estate values approached the figures reached at the height of the boom. In 1889, after the collapse of the "Boom," Newport Beach, a bare strip of sand, came in for considerable attention and slow development into the prosperous city it is today.*

Finley's reminisces end on a positive note; once the rampant speculation of 1887 was over, the market was prepared for the founding of what would go on to be one of Orange County's most significant cities: Newport Beach.

Fighting the Bull

During the nineteenth century, several California counties (including Orange) were known as the "cow counties." While Los Angeles was often called the "Queen of the Cow Counties," Orange had its fair share of ranching. Andrew Joplin, a legend in the county's history and folklore, had a close encounter with a particularly ill-tempered bull in his youth.

> *Andrew Joplin relates that it was a favorite sport, in the days when Orange County was known as one of the "cow counties," for the young cowboys to fight or tease the bulls. One day when out riding with a group of young fellows, they met a bull on the "prod." They dared Joplin to fight it, and he couldn't take a dare. He then took off his coat and dismounted, faced the bull holding his coat at arm's length, waving it at the bull which promptly charged. Andrew nimbly stepped to one side and the bull rushed by but immediately turned and charged again, this time he wasn't so lucky for the bull stuck one horn through the sleeve of his coat and wrested it out of his hands; it made another quick turn and Andrew, after a quick fast run, managed to climb a tree close by, an eyelash ahead of the bull. The cowboys shouted and yelled in glee at his discomfort and joked him about it for some time after, but Andrew says that if he had been in any real danger they would have promptly roped the bull and prevented it from harming him in any way.*

More traditional Spanish bullfights were also a spectacle in Orange County during this time. When the Santa Fe Railroad completed its line to San Juan Capistrano in 1887, special trains were run every Sunday to bring people to the event, as Joplin himself recounted.

> *A corral is built and the bull turned loose in it. The bull stands still and looks around as if wondering what it's all about. A banderillero maneuvers around and flings a banderilla—a rosette dart—which strikes into the side of the bull. A lazador now makes a dash at him, seizes his tail and sloughs him around, another banderillo penetrates his side, to which is attached a bunch of fire crackers, then a brave picador valorously lights them and another picador bounces on his back and the toreador kicks him in the nose. The bull loses his patience and makes a rush at the toreador who runs and climbs over the fence. A lazador has the old boy by the hind leg and another by the fore leg and he is thrown on his back. He regains his feet and is again confronted by the toreador with his red flag, while banderilleros cover his rear and flank and ply their cruel darts and crackers. The bull makes another charge at the toreador who this time nimbly dodges the bull and springs on its back. On his feet again, the bull makes another rush at him and he runs to climb over the fence. This time, however, a Gringo disgusted*

with the show pushes him back into the ring where the waiting bull tosses him into the air. The grand toreador is so badly hurt that he is laid up for a month and the show is over.

Several of these terms are probably unfamiliar to a modern reader. The toreador was the main bullfighter, but he would often have a group of men assisting him in his battle. A banderillero would run on foot to try to place sharp-pointed banderillas—"little flags"—on the bull's shoulders. These darts, as Joplin described them, were intended to hinder the bull's movement while charging. A picador, on the other hand, rode on horseback while testing the bull with a lance—called a "pica"—to give the matador information on the bull's weaknesses. The lazador would assist the toreador with a lasso.

Another Orange County old-timer, Mort Hubbard, also had recollections of the bullfights at San Juan Capistrano.

Frequently, a purse containing money was tied to a bull's horns as a reward to whoever could obtain it after the bull was turned loose. After some time had been wasted in individual efforts, several men held onto his tail while another leaped on his back and secured the prize.

Another of Hubbard's stories has a much more morbid ending.

A bull fight took place in the upper part of town which was attended by a dense crowd of spectators. The diversion as usual was attended by various casualties. One hombre more imprudent than proficient, in an endeavor to perform some exploits on foot (which are usual at bull fights in Mexico and Lima) was caught and tossed high in the air a number of times by an infuriated bull. After some delay he was rescued and was taken from the ground in a lifeless state.

After being taken from the ground he showed signs of returning animation and on examination it was found that he had two ribs broken and several internal bruises. A number of horses were badly gored and some even to death. This branch of amusement was kept up for three days to the evident delight of the boys and to the great suffering and ruin of many a noble steed.

Although the thought of Spanish-style bullfighting in Orange County may seem crazy to modern sensibilities, during the nineteenth century it was an important part of the local culture. Less than a century before, the area had still been under Spanish rule, and the event was very popular both for locals and for visitors hoping to witness the spectacle. Fortunately for the bulls involved, the practice is now outlawed in the United States, but it is fascinating from a cultural point of view to realize how prevalent and persistent it once was in our history.

Chapter 8

GOSPEL SWAMP

The name "Gospel Swamp" referred to the swampy area that once existed in what is now Huntington Beach, Fountain Valley, Westminster and other surrounding areas. An 1873 newspaper article explained how the region got its name: "The swamp was originally settled by a number of families, among whom were more than the usual proportion of preachers, so the community was remarkable for their piety and church-going. Hence the name of the settlement."

Because this area was typically farmland and sparsely populated, there are not many stories about the region in the WPA's *Pioneer Tales*. Here, however, are two that shed on what this long-lost part of the county was once like.

From Texas to California on Foot

One of the most remarkable stories recounted in the WPA volume is the story of Henry Pankey's crossing of the American West, even making large portions of the journey on foot. Here, in its entirety, is his tale.

Henry S. Pankey related a very interesting story of his crossing the plains in coming to California in 1869. He was born in Mississippi, but as his father died when he was a year old, his mother moved back to her native state, Tennessee, where her parents were living. She married again and at the outbreak of the Civil War went to Arkansas and in 1865 to Texas.

In the spring of 1869, the family joined a train of emigrants consisting of 12 wagons and started across the plains for California.

His step-father soon found so much fault with his driving the ox-team that he decided to quit the trip and return to Texas. Occupants of the other wagons offered to take him on and persuaded him to stay with the train. When they reached the Rio Grande River, the train split up, half went on, the other half staying in camp.

There was another boy in camp about his own age. They were taking turns with the men in guarding the train at night against possible raids from Indians, who would run off their livestock and might kill the sleepers. The Comanches were on one side of the Rio Grande, the Apaches on the other. His pal was found asleep several times while on guard and was severely reprimanded by the boss of the train. He told his father that he was going to shoot the boss for picking on him, so when it was decided that he would have to leave the train, Pankey agreed to accompany him. Having two saddle horses, he loaned one to Pankey. They packed water bottles and some provisions in their saddle bags as it was 65 miles to the next place where they could find water, and started to overtake the part of their train that had gone on ahead.

As the Indians were so dangerous, the boys had to travel at night. It was so dark they couldn't see over 50 feet ahead. After a few hours his pal insisted that he had to have some sleep. Pankey pointed out that they must go through Cook's

Celery fields located in present-day Westminster during the early part of the twentieth century. Relatively undeveloped at the time, this was near the area known as "Gospel Swamp" for many years. *Courtesy the Orange County Archives.*

The Methodist Auditorium, located in what is now Huntington Beach, was part of what was formerly known as Gospel Swamp. During the first decade of the twentieth century, a tent city of devout Methodists sprang up around the auditorium. *Courtesy the Orange County Archives.*

Canyon at night as it was in this narrow dark canyon that the Indians most often ambushed travelers. He insisted, however, that he couldn't go on without some sleep. So they took the saddles off their horses, turned them loose, and had a short sleep. When they awoke it was so dark that they had a lot of trouble finding their horses. His pal, confused, wanted to go back the way they had come, but Pankey insisted on the opposite direction, for, before going to sleep, he had taken the precaution of pointing his saddle in the direction they were to go. About daybreak, they overtook the train and were hired to help a man who had taken 100 head of cattle to Tucson. They were to receive $10.00 and board for the job. At this point his companion became peeved with him and took back his horse, so Pankey had to herd the cattle on foot.

When they reached Tucson, Pankey with four other boys were paid off. They had two horses, and $10 each, so they started out, two mounted and three afoot. When they reached the Gila River, he got a job on a ranch and worked until able to buy a pony, then started for Yuma seventy miles further on.

The first night, he fell in with a man who had a team of mules and who talked him into selling him his pony. He finished the trip to Yuma, 35 miles, on foot.

Here, having spent all of his money for another little horse, he went to the Government Barracks, told his story and was given an old saddle. At the

Barracks they told him if he would be at the ferry in the morning, when the stage went over, he would be able to get across the Colorado River without it costing him anything. This he did, proceeding on to San Diego County, stopped at Campo, near Indian Wells, and went to work chopping wood. Almost the first day he cut his foot so badly with the ax that he was laid up for some time. A man came along about this time and asked him if he would go to Los Angeles with him if given expenses. He agreed, but at Lake Elsinore the man told him he was going to stay there and that he had better keep on going.

When night overtook him, he had found no place to stop, but finally saw a light and came to a little house. It was occupied by an old Spanish woman. He showed her his empty pocket book, and was invited in, given some beans and jerky and a sheep skin to sleep on. In the morning she gave him breakfast and he was again on his way.

He soon overtook another young fellow who was going to Los Angeles, so they travelled together. At the Temescal Canyon the road forked. They took the wrong road until they met a Jewish peddler who told them they could follow down the river and save going back to the forks. They had nothing to eat that day and at night slept along the river.

In the morning they came to the home of one of the Yorbas who had nothing but bread, which was shared with them. The boys had nothing more to eat that day. At night they slept in a mustard field. Next morning they reached El Monte where an Irishman in charge of the stage depot gave them a fine breakfast of ham and eggs and coffee. Pankey proceeded to Azusa and after two or three days went to work on a ranch. The employer didn't have any money but agreed that if he would work six months he would receive his board and a horse. After completing this contract, he got two months work haying for which he was paid $50.00.

All of this time he had heard nothing of what had become of his mother. When he received the $50.00 he came to the Old Gallatin. There was a saloon there and a lot of horses tied up in the front. He thought he recognized one of the saddles so hunted up the owner and asked him where he got that saddle. The man replied, "From the Clarks, what about it?" "Nothing," he replied, "except Mrs. Clark is my mother and I am looking for her." He was shown where she, again a widow, was living, and there was a real joyful reunion.

In 1874 Pankey came to Orange County and bought 40 acres southeast of Westminster from the Stearns Ranch company at $30 an acre. The place had some peat land and was so swampy that the horses that walked in the furrows, when plowing, had to be equipped with wooden boards about 8 x 10 x 12 inches attached to their feet to prevent them from miring *down. He had wonderful crops; over 100 bushels of corn to the care and pumpkins so large that he had to have help to put them in a wagon. He raised lots of hogs, once paying $50 an acre for a corn crop to feed them.*

His hogs sold from 2½¢ to 5¢ a pound. They furnished him with hams, bacon, and lard for his own use. He also farmed for a while on the San Joaquin Ranch. He rented and farmed 1,000 acres where the city of Huntington Beach is located. So many wild geese came in the fall and stayed there all winter that he had to drive around and shoot to scare them away from the fields. Sometimes they would entirely cover a 40-acre field. Although he was offered this land at $8 an acre, he bought 100 acres near Talbert for $30 an acre and started a dairy. He was quite successful until the Texas ticks got into his herd and most of the cattle died of what was called the Texas Fever.

This place had a wonderful spring, which boiled up and formed a little river. It was so deep that when his horses got into it they would drown, being unable to get out. The place had to be drained before it could be tilled.

He owned a fine stallion named Comet, although it only weighed 1,100 pounds. His colts were so pretty and had such fine dispositions and intelligence that he became a favorite among stock raisers.

Some Pumpkins!

Since its earliest days, Orange County has been renowned for its fertile farmland. At various times, the region has been known for its avocados, walnuts, chili peppers and, obviously, oranges. One crop not often associated with the county is pumpkins, although the following tale proves that Orange County's rich soil was more than suitable for them. The story begins in Santa Barbara.

A pumpkin was on exhibition at the Santa Barbara Fair in the Fall about 1890. A hole had been cut in the top, the seeds removed and in the center, seated in comfort, was the belle of the County. She was busy selling tickets, at twenty-five cents each, which entitled the purchaser to a guess as to the number of pies that she could make out of the mammoth pumpkin. The person making the best guess won a handsome prize, provided he had also placed an order for one of the lady's famous pies. A large sum of money was raised for a very worthy cause, but the claim that this was the largest pumpkin ever raised in the State started many arguments, which resulted in a lot of pumpkin heads being punched without settling the momentous question.

While not as large as the alleged largest pumpkin in the world, this whimsical photograph shows one of Orange County's early pumpkin crops. *Courtesy the Santa Ana Public Library.*

In lieu of the argument over California's largest pumpkin, one old-timer recalled an anecdote from the 1890s about a giant he had seen at a farm in Orange County. Mr. Joshua J. Pyle, the man he came to visit, was one of the "most successful and highly regarded citizens" in Orange County at the time. Born in Pennsylvania, Pyle moved to California in 1885 and began farming a tract of land near Westminster. He lived there with his wife for forty-six years, during which time he became prominent in a number of local civic organizations. The story of Mr. Pyle's pumpkins is as follows.

> *A winter visitor to Orange County, who had seen the two-hundred pound pumpkin raised by Mr. Joshua Pyle and sent to the Chicago World's Fair for exhibition related the following incident. He had called one morning at the Jerico Ranch, and had found the owner, Mr. Pyle, worrying over the strange disappearance of his favorite brood sow. The two men made a careful examination of the hog-tight fence but failed to find any place where she could have escaped. It was then decided to make a thorough search through the corn field. The corn was so tall that the stalks had to be cut down in order to harvest the crop—the ears growing too high to be reached on foot. Between the rows of corn, pumpkins had been planted, a crop of large ones raised which were ready to be gathered.*
>
> *After considerable time had been spent in searching, they noticed a hole in the side of one of the largest of the pumpkins in the field and on looking in the hole they discovered the lost sow nursing her newly arrived family of ten little piggies.*

While a 200-pound pumpkin may seem impressive, the record for the world's largest pumpkin was set by a California farmer in 2013. Its weight? 2,032 pounds.

INDEX

ABOUT THE EDITOR

Born in Santa Monica and raised in Huntington Beach, California, Charles Epting is an undergraduate student at the University of Southern California. He is studying history and geology. For several years, he has been a volunteer at the Los Angeles County Museum of Natural History, studying paleontology. He is the author of *University Park, Los Angeles* and *The New Deal in Orange County*.